FAITHFULNESS

WALKING IN THE LIGHT

AT A GLANCE

Serendipity House / P.O. Box 1012 / Littleton, CO 80160
TOLL FREE 1-800-525-9563 / www.serendipityhouse.com
© 1989, 1998 Serendipity House. All rights reserved.
SECOND EDITION
99 00 01 02 / **201 series • CHG** / 5 4 3 2

PROJECT ENGINEER:
Lyman Coleman

WRITING TEAM:
Richard Peace, Lyman Coleman, Matthew Lockhart, Andrew Sloan, Cathy Tardif

PRODUCTION TEAM:
Christopher Werner, Sharon Penington, Erika Tiepel

COVER PHOTO:
© 1998 Dean Dunson / Westlight

CORE VALUES

Community: The purpose of this curriculum is to build community within the body of believers around Jesus Christ.

Group Process: To build community, the curriculum must be designed to take a group through a step-by-step process of sharing your story with one another.

Interactive Bible Study: To share your "story," the approach to Scripture in the curriculum needs to be open-ended and right brain—to "level the playing field" and encourage everyone to share.

Developmental Stages: To provide a healthy program in the life cycle of a group, the curriculum needs to offer courses on three levels of commitment: (1) Beginner Stage—low-level entry, high structure, to level the playing field; (2) Growth Stage—deeper Bible study, flexible structure, to encourage group accountability; (3) Discipleship Stage—in-depth Bible study, open structure, to move the group into high gear.

Target Audiences: To build community throughout the culture of the church, the curriculum needs to be flexible, adaptable and transferable into the structure of the average church.

ACKNOWLEDGMENTS

To Zondervan Bible Publishers
for permission to use
the NIV text,
The Holy Bible, New International Bible Society.
© 1973, 1978, 1984 by International Bible Society.
Used by permission of Zondervan Bible Publishers.

Questions & Answers

STAGE

1. What stage in the life cycle of a small group is this course designed for?

Turn to the first page of the center section of this book. There you will see that this 201 course is designed for the second stage of a small group. In the Serendipity "Game Plan" for the multiplication of small groups, your group is in the Growth Stage.

GOALS

2. What are the goals of a 201 study course?

As shown on the second page of the center section (page M2), the focus in this second stage is equally balanced between Bible Study, Group Building, and Mission / Multiplication.

BIBLE STUDY

3. What is the approach to Bible Study in this course?

Take a look at page M3 of the center section. The objective in a 201 course is to discover what a book of the Bible, or a series of related Scripture passages, has to say to our lives today. We will study each passage seriously, but with a strong emphasis on practical application to daily living.

THREE-STAGE LIFE CYCLE OF A GROUP

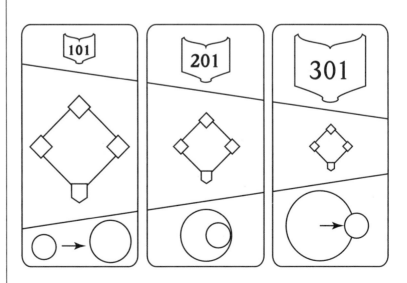

GROUP BUILDING

4. ***What is the meaning of the baseball diamond on pages M2 and M3 in relation to Group Building?***

    Every Serendipity course includes group building. First base is where we share our own stories; second base means affirming one another's stories; third base is sharing our personal needs; and home plate is deeply caring for each others' needs. In this 201 course we will continue "checking in" with each other and holding each other accountable to live the Christian life.

MISSION / MULTIPLICATION

5. ***What is the mission of a 201 group?***

    The mission of this 201 Covenant group is to discover the future leaders for starting a new group. (See graph on the previous page.) During this course, you will be challenged to identify three people and let this team use the Bible Study time to practice their skills. The center section will give you more details.

THE EMPTY CHAIR

6. ***How do we fill "the empty chair"?***

    First, pull up an empty chair during the group's prayer time and ask God to bring a new person to the group to fill it. Second, have everyone make a prospect list of people they could invite and keep this list on their refrigerator until they have contacted all those on their list.

AGENDA

7. ***What is the agenda for our group meetings?***

    A three-part agenda is found at the beginning of each session. Following the agenda and the recommended amount of time will keep your group on track and will keep the three goals of Bible Study, Group Building, and Mission / Multiplication in balance.

THE FEARLESS FOURSOME

If you have more than seven people at a meeting, Serendipity recommends you divide into groups of 4 for the Bible Study. Count off around the group: "one, two, one, two, etc."—and have the "ones" move quickly to another room for the Bible Study. Ask one person to be the leader and follow the directions for the Bible Study time. After 30 minutes, the Group Leader will call "Time" and ask all groups to come together for the Caring Time.

8. ***How do we decide what ice-breakers to use to begin the meetings?***

Page M7 of the center section contains an index of ice-breakers in four categories: (1) those for getting acquainted in the first session or when a new person comes to a meeting; (2) those for the middle sessions to help you report in to your group; (3) those for the latter sessions to affirm each other and assign roles in preparation for starting a new group in the future; and (4) those for evaluating and reflecting in the final session.

9. ***What is a group covenant?***

A group covenant is a "contract" that spells out your expectations and the ground rules for your group. It's very important that your group discuss these issues—preferably as part of the first session (see also page M32 in the center section).

10. ***What are the ground rules for the group?*** (Check those you agree upon.)

❏ PRIORITY: While you are in the course, you give the group meetings priority.

❏ PARTICIPATION: Everyone participates and no one dominates.

❏ RESPECT: Everyone is given the right to their own opinion and all questions are encouraged and respected.

❏ CONFIDENTIALITY: Anything that is said in the meeting is never repeated outside the meeting.

❏ EMPTY CHAIR: The group stays open to new people at every meeting.

❏ SUPPORT: Permission is given to call upon each other in time of need—even in the middle of the night.

❏ ADVICE GIVING: Unsolicited advice is not allowed.

❏ MISSION: We agree to do everything in our power to start a new group as our mission (see center section).

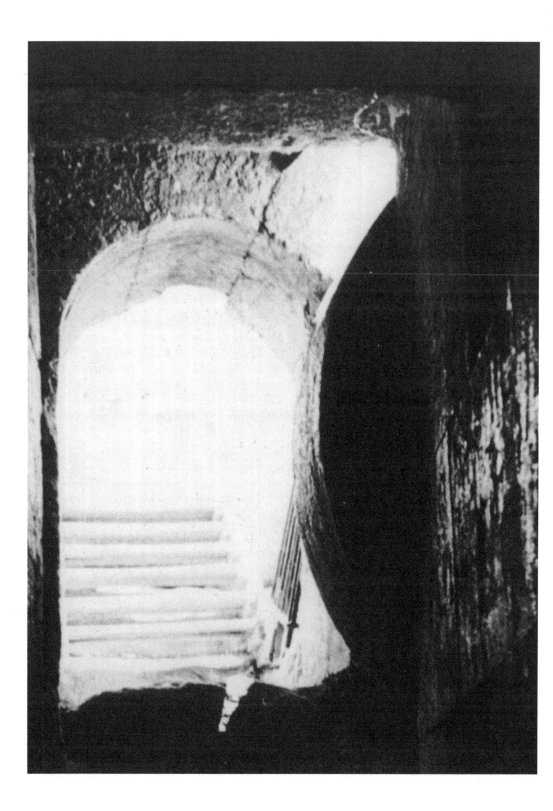

Introduction to 1 John

John was an old man when he wrote his first epistle. All the other disciples were dead. Only he remained of the original Twelve. His long life had afforded him the opportunity to witness the spectacular growth of the church. It had begun with only a handful of disciples clustered together in Jerusalem. Now Christianity had spread throughout the known world, and the believers had become so numerous that it was difficult to number them all.

But not all that John had seen was good. As well as growth, there had been dissension, defection, and heresy—even in the churches John pastored. In fact, this is why he came to write this epistle: a group of people from his church had gotten involved in strange doctrine. They had then left the church and formed their own community. Now they were trying to persuade other Christians to do the same thing—to leave and join this new group.

So John was compelled to write this letter. In fact, it had become an urgent need. Soon, like the other apostles, his time would be at an end. And when he was gone, who would ensure that the church remained loyal to the teachings of Jesus? It was vital that the church understand clearly what lay at the heart of Christianity. It was vital that Christians grasp firmly the nature of the Gospel.

So John wrote his first epistle. In it one gets the sense that here John is boiling down the Gospel to its essence: "God is Light; God is Love; Jesus is the Messiah, the Son of God who has come in the flesh; and we are to be his children who have eternal life, who do not continue in sin, and who love one another." This is what it is all about. This is what God has been trying to teach the human race for all these hundreds of years. Here John is distilling all the wisdom and insight of his long years into a few incisive chapters. In the First Epistle of John, therefore, what we have is essential Christianity as seen by the last of the Twelve. John records here his final thoughts on the nature of the faith so that, once and for all, we would get it straight. As such, John's epistle is the summation of revelation history and thus it is a book to master—with both heart and head.

Occasion

There were problems in John's church—deep ones that compelled him to write. It is difficult, of course, to reconstruct with full accuracy just what the situation was in the multiple house churches in the Ephesus area where John ministered. Still, it appears that what happened was that a group of Christians got involved in false teaching, split off from the church (2:19), and then started hassling their former friends, probably trying to convince them to espouse their new, "advanced" religious views (2:26). (This is a typical response. If you can get others to agree with your newly embraced viewpoint, then you yourself feel more confident that you are, indeed, "right.") Thus, John writes this epistle to refute these erroneous views and to encourage those in the church to remain faithful to the Gospel as taught by the apostles.

The error of these secessionists was twofold: they had a defective view of Jesus and a wrong view of sin. On their view of Jesus, they were so caught up with the idea of Jesus as the divine, pre-existent Lord that they almost totally neglected his human side. While they probably would not deny that Jesus was a man, to them this fact was insignificant. His humanity did not really matter in comparison with his divinity. As a result, they did not believe Jesus to be the Messiah (2:22; 5:1). In particular, they denied that Jesus, as the Son of God, had died. This was the really fatal error, because it cuts to the very heart of the Gospel. Since God is love and since love is the laying down of one's life (John 15:13), if the Son of God did not die then God has not been revealed in Christ.

They also had an erroneous view of ethics. Specifically, they claimed to be free from sin, and free from the commandment to love others. Since they did not confess that Jesus was the

Messiah, they did not feel any need to obey what he said. And since they felt that they were free from sin, they did not need the Son of God to die in their place for their sins.

These secessionists had come to think of themselves as some sort of spiritual "elite," claiming (probably by direct revelation—see 4:1–6) that they had a "deeper" understanding of Christianity than others. As an antidote to this sort of spiritual pride, John reminds his readers again and again that Christians are called upon to love one another. They are not to look down on those brothers and sisters who do not measure up to their own (supposed) superior insight.

It is not clear what, if any, "label" can be affixed to this group of secessionists. The ideas they held were probably related to what later became Gnosticism—a philosophy that taught that matter (including the body) was impure and that the "spirit" was all that really counted. Therefore, it is not surprising that these secessionists, with this Gnostic view of reality, minimized the humanity of Jesus. To them salvation came via illumination. Thus esoteric "knowledge" is what they sought, instead of hearing and heeding apostolic doctrine.

Authorship

But did the apostle John actually write this epistle? This has been the assumption thus far in these notes. Yet there are those scholars who would question whether this is so.

In fact, the author of this letter is nowhere named in 1 John. So, whatever one concludes, it is by way of speculation. However, a good case can be made that John, the beloved apostle, is indeed the author of this epistle. There are a number of reasons for attributing this anonymous epistle to him, including:

1. The strong tradition dating back to the early days of the church that John was the author.

2. The many similarities in style and content between the Gospel of John and this epistle. The same sharp contrasts appear in both—between light and darkness; truth and falsehood; love and hate. What differences do exist between the two books can be traced to differences in purpose arising out of differences in audience, since the historical context had shifted between the time of the Gospel and the time of this epistle.

3. The internal information in the epistle points to John as the author. For example, the author tells us that he was one of the original eyewitnesses of Jesus (1:1–2). Also, the author writes with the air of authority that would be expected of one who was an apostle (see 4:6).

Date

It is very difficult to fix a date to this epistle. The evidence is not clear nor conclusive. However, the best guess is that 1 John was written toward the end of the New Testament era (A.D. 90–95), by which time this gnostic-like heresy had begun to flourish.

Style

First John is written in the simplest Greek found in all the New Testament. (It is the first book seminary students learn to translate.) There are 5,437 different Greek words that appear in the New Testament, yet in the three Johannine epistles, only 303 of these are used—5 1/2 percent of the total. This is not to say, however, that 1 John is a simple, superficial book. On the contrary, it is one of the most profound books in the entire New Testament. Perhaps because of (not despite) his simple vocabulary, John focuses in on the core of the Gospel. All else is cut away. He writes only what really matters.

A story is told by Jerome about the "blessed John the evangelist" when he was an extremely old man. According to Jerome, John now has to be carried into the worship service at Ephesus. John is unable to say anything except "little children, love one another," which he repeats over and over. The believers, having heard this same thing so often, ask: "Master, why do you always say this?" "Because," he replied, "it is enough."

Martin Luther wrote: "I have never read a book written in simpler words than this one, and yet the words are inexpressible."

Literary Form

First John is not an epistle in the sense that 2 and 3 John are (or in the sense of Paul's letters). It does not identify the writer or the recipients. In fact, there is no specific name or place mentioned anywhere in this document. There is no salutation nor is there a final greeting. It is clear that this is intentional, since John knew perfectly well how a letter was written. 3 John has been called by some the most perfect example in the New Testament of Greek letter format. Clearly, here John was writing a different sort of document.

Three things are evident about John's effort here. First, this is a literary document. John states some 13 times that he is writing (in contrast to speaking or preaching; see, for example, 1:4). And, second, it is clear that he has a specific audience in mind, which he refers to as "you" (in the plural) some 22 times. Third, there is a so-called "double-opening" (similar to that in James), within which John states twice the themes he then develops in the rest of the manuscript. So what we have here is probably a "literary epistle"—a written document addressed to a particular audience. His audience is the community of churches in and around Ephesus that he pastored and which remained loyal to the Gospel he preached.

Structure and Theme

It is difficult to "outline" 1 John; i.e., to track the flow of the author's thought and put it into neat categories and divisions (as one can do with Romans, for example). Rather, it seems that John (much like James) would write a paragraph and then be reminded of a related topic which he would then deal with in the next paragraph. This, in turn, would spark a further thought. This is not to say that John's ideas tumble out in a haphazard fashion. This is certainly not the case. His ideas are focused and interrelated. The ideas hang together—but not by means of a western style of logic. The structure is almost spiral, "for the development of a theme often brings us back almost to the starting-point; almost but not quite, for there is a slight shift which provides a transition to a fresh theme; or it may be to a theme which had apparently been dismissed at an earlier point and now comes up for consideration from a slightly different angle" (Dodd).

John's central concern is quite clear, however. He wants to define the marks of a true Christian, over against what was being taught by the secessionists. This is very important. He wants his congregation to have the assurance that they do, indeed, have eternal life (5:13), despite what the false teachers are saying. What, then, are these "marks"? According to John Stott, the characteristics of a true Christian in 1 John are these: right belief (the doctrinal test), righteousness (the moral test), and love (the social test).

1 The Word of Life—1 John 1:1–4

THREE-PART AGENDA

ICE-BREAKER
15 Minutes

BIBLE STUDY
30 Minutes

CARING TIME
15–45 Minutes

> *LEADER: Be sure to read pages 3–5 in the front of this book, and go over the ground rules on page 5 with the group in this first session. See page M7 in the center section for a good ice-breaker. Have your group look at pages M1–M5 in the center section and fill out the team roster on page M5.*

TO BEGIN THE BIBLE STUDY TIME
(Choose 1 or 2)

1. Where were your parents living when you were born? Growing up, how many times did your family move?

2. What hobby or activity adds joy to your life?

3. What inspires you: Beautiful music? Breathtaking scenery? Other?

READ SCRIPTURE & DISCUSS
(If you don't have time for all the questions in this section, conclude the Bible Study [30 min.] by answering question #7.)

1. When have you had an experience that you couldn't wait to tell someone else about?

2. Why is John able to testify to what Jesus said and did? What does this mean to you as you start this study?

3. What is John referring to "concerning the Word of life" (see last note on v. 1)?

The Word of Life

1 *That which was from the beginning, which we have heard, which we have seen with our eyes, which we have looked at and our hands have touched—this we proclaim concerning the Word of life. ²The life appeared; we have seen it and testify to it, and we proclaim to you the eternal life, which was with the Father and has appeared to us. ³We proclaim to you what we have seen and heard, so that you also may have fellowship with us. And our fellowship is with the Father and with his Son, Jesus Christ. ⁴We write this to make our[a] joy complete.*

[a]4 Some manuscripts *your*

P.S. At the close, pass around your books and have everyone sign the Group Directory inside the front cover.

4. From this passage, what are some reasons John wrote this epistle?

5. When have you been part of a group where you enjoyed true fellowship—where there was mutual love and understanding?

6. On a scale of 1 (don't ask) to 10 (my cup runneth over), how much joy did you experience this past week?

7. What brought you to this study and what are you hoping to get out of it?

CARING TIME

1. Have your group agree on the group covenant and ground rules (see page 5 in the front of this book).

2. Work on filling out your team roster (see page M5 in the center section). Like any winning team, every position needs to be covered.

3. Who is someone you would like to invite to this group for next week?

Share prayer requests and close in prayer. Be sure to pray for "the empty chair" (p. 4).

Notes—1 John 1:1–4

Summary. John begins his letter with a prologue that is reminiscent of the prologue to his Gospel (John 1:1–18). Both prologues focus on the pre-existent Word of God who has been revealed to humanity. But there are also differences between the two. In the Gospel prologue, the emphasis is on the divine nature of the Word. In this prologue, the emphasis is on the *physical manifestation* of the Word of God. This difference is due to the difference in audiences. In his Gospel, John wrote to Jews who did not believe that God could reveal himself in the person of Jesus. But here, the secessionists presuppose that Jesus is the Son of God. Their problem is that they neglect his human side. This is why John emphasizes the fact that the pre-existent Word has been experienced by auditory, visual and manual means. Although this prologue is only four verses long, it is a complex piece of writing. In Greek, this is a single sentence which is, according to one scholar, a "grammatical tangle" (Dodd). The structure has a distinct purpose—John focuses attention on the object which is proclaimed (Jesus Christ), rather than on the act of proclamation itself.

> *John's point is that fellowship with God is possible only through Jesus, because in him eternal life (i.e., God's life) is manifested.*

1:1 Although this document lacks the usual identification of sender and recipient (as well as the normal greeting and prayer), it is clear that this is not an anonymous tract written to a general audience. Scattered throughout the letter are abundant personal comments and specific references (e.g., 2:19; 3:2).

which. John begins with four clauses, each introduced by "which." The first clause describes who the "Word of life" is. The next three describe how he was experienced.

from the beginning. The initial clause makes the astonishing assertion that this "Word of life" was pre-existent (see John 1:1). Since only divine beings pre-existed, John affirms Jesus' deity.

heard / seen / touched. However, John's emphasis is on the human nature of Jesus. The next three clauses describe how his physical presence was experienced. Notice the progression: in the Old Testament, men and women had *heard* God on many occasions; occasionally they had *seen* some aspect of God (see Ex. 3:1–6; 33:18–23); but no one had ever *touched* God. This was the final proof that the Word of life had indeed been "made flesh and dwelt among us" (John 1:14, KJV). In Greek courts, the testimony of two senses was required in order to verify that something occurred (Brown). John offers evidence from a third sense as well.

touched. This word means literally "to feel after" or "to grope," as a blind person might do. It also means "to examine closely" (Brooke).

Word of life. The message preached by the apostles and by Jesus himself concerned eternal life (i.e., spiritual life). This is one sense of the phrase "Word of life." But Jesus not only preached this message. He *was* the message. This is the second sense of the phrase (see John 1:4; 11:25–26; 14:6).

1:2 This is a parenthesis in which John declares in unequivocal terms that *Jesus* is the Word he is talking about.

The life appeared. The One who is the creator of all life entered into life. The author's authority rests on the fact that he was an eyewitness to this revelation of God.

we. The author is among those who knew Jesus personally.

testify. This is a legal term describing what an eyewitness does while in court. Such a person makes a public declaration of what he or she has experienced firsthand.

eternal life. John focuses on what is so significant about Jesus: he is life itself. God's very life has appeared in the historical person of Jesus (see John 1:2).

1:3 *We proclaim.* This is the main verb of the opening sentence. It clarifies the intention of the prologue. John's aim is to identify the nature of the apostolic proclamation, which is that Jesus is the incarnate God.

> *Joy is the profound gladness or satisfaction that comes when one participates in the life of God.*

fellowship. This word means literally, in Greek, "having in common." It has the dual sense of *participation together* in shared activity or outlook, and *union together* because of this shared experience. John's purpose is to bring others into participation and union with him and his colleagues, and thus into participation and union with the Father and the Son.

with the Father and with his Son. Apparently the false teachers were saying that it was possible to have fellowship with God apart from Christ. John's point is that fellowship with God is possible only through Jesus (2:23), because in him eternal life (i.e., God's life) is manifested.

1:4 John identifies his second reason for writing. He wants his own joy to be completed.

joy. This is the profound gladness or satisfaction that comes when one participates in the life of God. It is an important term for John. He uses it nine times in his Gospel (along with an additional nine times that he uses the verb "rejoice"). See, for example, John 15:11; 16:20,22,24 and 17:13, each of which promises joy. In John 20:20 he indicates that the fulfillment of this promise is found in the experience of the resurrected Lord. Here in 1 John he goes one step further and indicates the joy which began with the experience of the resurrected Lord is brought to completion via the experience of this full-orbed fellowship between Father, Son and the children of God. The children of God include the apostles and those who have believed the good news which they proclaimed about Jesus.

complete. Full, lacking nothing.

Seeing is believing ...
But touching is better

When John says that they not only heard and saw Jesus, but actually touched him, we understand what he is saying. He is asserting in the strongest possible experiential language that Jesus had a real body. Jesus was no phantom or will-of-the-wisp. He was not "materialized spirit." He was not an allusion. He was real like we are real. His was a flesh-and-blood body with smooth skin, real muscles, eyes that stared back at you, and with hair that had to be combed.

It is necessary for John to make this point because of the secessionists who are troubling his church. They wanted their Jesus to be fully divine. They wanted God. They were not so sure about man. Of course, they knew that Jesus had been a man—sort of. But this is not what they liked about Jesus. What they liked was his deity and all he could teach them about the supernatural.

The problem with their view (it was later labeled docetism and condemned as a heresy) was that in downplaying Jesus' humanity, they minimized his atoning work. They minimized his dying for sins. They minimized sin. And so this view could not be allowed to stand. If Jesus did not die for our sins as a real man (who was sinless) then we are still in sin—cut off from God and lost. This was no minor theological error. This is the kind of misunderstanding that undercut the very heart of Christianity.

It is important to know this. Two thousand years later there are those folk among us who say that the American church has once again become docetic. We don't deny Jesus was human, but the fact is that what we like most about him is his divinity. This is still a problem. In losing sight of his humanity we cut ourselves off from all that he can teach us about our own struggle to become fully human.

2 Walking in Light—1 John 1:5–2:2

THREE-PART AGENDA

ICE-BREAKER	BIBLE STUDY	CARING TIME
15 Minutes	30 Minutes	15–45 Minutes

 LEADER: If there's a new person in your group in this session, start with an ice-breaker (see page M7 in the center section). Then begin the session with a word of prayer. If you have more than seven in your group, see the box about the "Fearless Foursome" on page 4. Count off around the group: "one, two, one, two, etc."—and have the "ones" move quickly to another room for the Bible Study.

TO BEGIN THE BIBLE STUDY TIME
(Choose 1 or 2)

1. Growing up, what did your parents do to help you not be afraid of the dark?

2. What is your favorite kind of light: Sunlight? Neon light? Starlight? Night-light? Firelight? Flashlight? Other?

3. How do you keep in touch with family and friends who don't live near you?

READ SCRIPTURE & DISCUSS
(If you don't have time for all the questions in this section, conclude the Bible Study [30 min.] by answering question #7.)

1. Who is someone who has been a good example to you of how to live?

2. What does it mean to "walk in darkness" (v. 6)? How can we "walk in the light" (v. 7)?

Walking in the Light

⁵This is the message we have heard from him and declare to you: God is light; in him there is no darkness at all. ⁶If we claim to have fellowship with him yet walk in the darkness, we lie and do not live by the truth. ⁷But if we walk in the light, as he is in the light, we have fellowship with one another, and the blood of Jesus, his Son, purifies us from all^a sin.

⁸If we claim to be without sin, we deceive ourselves and the truth is not in us. ⁹If we confess our sins, he is faithful and just and will forgive us our sins and purify us from all unrighteousness. ¹⁰If we claim we have not sinned, we make him out to be a liar and his word has no place in our lives.

2 *My dear children, I write this to you so that you will not sin. But if anybody does sin, we have one who speaks to the Father in our defense—Jesus Christ, the Righteous One. ²He is the atoning sacrifice for our sins, and not only for ours but also for^b the sins of the whole world.*

^a7 Or every   ^b2 Or He is the one who turns aside God's wrath, taking away our sins, and not only ours but also

3. In practical terms, what does walking in the light look like?

4. What false claims does John dispute in this passage?

5. When we sin, what can we do to "clean up"? What are the pitfalls of denying the sin within us?

6. How does it make you feel to know that Jesus speaks to God "in our defense" (v. 1)?

7. What is one way you can walk in the light this week?

P.S. Add new group members to the Group Directory inside the front cover.

CARING TIME
(Choose 1 or 2 of these questions before closing in prayer. Be sure to pray for the empty chair.)

1. Who did you invite to the group this week? Who would you like to invite to the next meeting to fill "the empty chair"?

2. If you were to describe the last week of your life in terms of weather, what was it like: Sunny and warm? Cold? Scattered showers? Other? What is the forecast for the coming week?

3. How can the group pray for you this week?

Notes—1 John 1:5–2:2

Summary. In the prologue, John declares his hope that all may be in fellowship with God and with each other. Here in these verses, he examines the barrier that prevents such fellowship (i.e., sin) and how to deal with it. By means of a series of "if/then" clauses (with the "then" implied) he identifies three erroneous views of sin which he then evaluates on the basis of the fact that God is light. His pattern of writing is to begin a sentence with "if" and then state the false view and its detrimental consequences (vv. 6,8,10). He then starts a new sentence, again with the word "if," within which he states the correct view (vv. 7,9; 2:1b).

1:5 *God is light.* This is John's second great assertion about God. His first assertion was that *God had come in the flesh* (vv. 1–3). Here he states that *God is light*. Within contemporary Greek culture, "light" was a common symbol for God. It conveyed the idea of wisdom, integrity, excellence, etc. Within the context of the Bible, "light" was connected to two basic ideas. First, on the intellectual level, it was a symbol of truth. John is saying that God is truth. God illuminates the understanding of people. He reveals the right answer and the correct way (see Ps. 27:1 and Prov. 6:23). Second, on the moral level, light is a symbol of purity. John is saying that God is righteous and holy (see Isa. 5:20; Rom. 13:11–14 and Eph. 5:8–14). He is good, not evil. The coming of Jesus was, therefore, the coming of light (see Matt. 4:16; John 1:4–9 and 3:19–21). Jesus is "the light," as John states in his Gospel. He is the incarnation of the divine light (John 8:12; 9:5). This insight into the nature of God stands in sharp contrast to the many "dark gods" known in the first-century world who were given over more to evil than to good.

> *The granting of forgiveness is not merely an act of unanticipated mercy but a response of justice, since the conditions for forgiveness have been fulfilled as a result of the death of Christ.*

1:6 *If we claim.* The first of three false claims that John will refute. He will measure the validity of each against the apostolic proclamation that God is light and in him is no darkness.

to have fellowship ... yet walk in the darkness. It is claimed by the false teachers that it is possible to be in union with God and yet habitually sin. But if God is *light,* then by definition, those who walk in *darkness* cannot be part of him. This was a common error. It was felt that since the body was insignificant, it did not matter what a person did. The true essence of the person—the "spirit"—remained untouched and thus uncontaminated by sin.

we lie. John moves from the false proposition (that they have fellowship with God even while living in darkness) to the inevitable conclusion (they are not telling the truth). To say that one can practice sin and still be in fellowship with God is simply not true.

1:7 *But if.* Having identified the false proposition of the secessionists in verse 6, John now states the true proposition in verse 7.

walk in the light. The image here is of a person confidently striding forth, illuminated by the light of God's truth, in contrast to the person who stumbles around in darkness.

purifies. If the first result of "walking in the light" is fellowship with one another, the second result is cleansing from sin. The verb tense indicates that this purification occurs not just once, but is a continuous process.

1:8 *If we claim to be without sin.* The second false claim: that they are sinless. It is one thing to deny that sin breaks fellowship with God (as in vv. 6–7). At least then the existence of sin is admitted (even if its impact is denied); but it is another thing to deny the fact of sin altogether. This might have been the response of the secessionists to John's assertion (in v. 6) that because they walked in the darkness of sin they could have no fellowship with God. "But," they would protest, "this cannot be sin. In fact, we have no sin at all." They might claim that they are without sin for one of two reasons: either because they felt that sin had to do with the body and the body had nothing to do with "fellowship with God." (One fellowshipped with God via the "spirit" and by their own definition, no sin could or did taint their spirit.) Or they could have felt that as a result of the special esoteric knowledge they had about God, they had been cleansed from all sin and granted perfected natures.

we deceive ourselves. This assertion goes beyond a mere lie (v. 6). This is self-deception. They really believed they were without sin.

the truth is not in us. Not only do they not live by the truth (v. 6), but by such a claim they demonstrate that they do not even know the truth (as found, for example in Rom. 3:23—"all have sinned.") Again, this demonstrates that they are not part of God, who is light, and who therefore stands for truth.

1:9 If we confess our sins. After naming the problem, John states the antidote. Rather than denying their sinful natures, they need to admit their sin to God and so gain forgiveness.

faithful. God will keep his promise to forgive (Mic. 7:18–20).

just. The granting of forgiveness is not merely an act of unanticipated mercy but a response of justice, since the conditions for forgiveness have been fulfilled as a result of the death of Christ.

purify. Sin makes a person unclean; forgiveness washes away that sin (see v. 7).

1:10 If we claim we have not sinned. The third false claim: not only do they say that at the present moment they are without sin (v. 8), they actually claim never to have sinned! The false teachers might admit that sin does break fellowship with God (v. 6) and that all people have an inborn sinful nature (v. 8), but they would still deny that they, in fact, have ever actually sinned.

we make him out to be a liar. God's verdict is that all people are sinners. Furthermore, he says that it is through the death of Christ that he forgives sin. By claiming sinlessness they are, in essence, saying that God is lying about human nature and about his claim to forgive people.

his word has no place in our lives. They claim to know God and yet they do not walk in his way nor accept his viewpoint about human nature. Therefore, contrary to what they might claim, they are, in fact, alienated from God (see John 8:44).

> ### God will keep his promise to forgive.

2:1–2 Here is the antidote to the third and final error of John's opponents. John alters the structure of his sentence slightly by placing the "if" in the middle of his statement and not at the beginning, but it is clear that he is responding to the assertion that they have never sinned.

2:1 dear children. This is literally "small children," an affectionate term for his congregation which John uses frequently (2:12,28; 3:7,18; 4:4; 5:21). At this point in his letter John shifts his focus from the secessionists and their heresy to his own flock and their needs.

so that you will not sin. Having just stated that Christians are not free from sin (v. 10), John runs the risk of being misinterpreted. People might say, "Since sin is always with us and since forgiveness is freely offered, then why not sin?" (see Rom. 6:1). Thus, John quickly points out that sin is not compatible with Christian commitment.

if anybody does sin. While urging sinlessness as a goal to strive for, John knows that in this present life this cannot be achieved. So the issue then is how to deal with sin. The answer is found in the triple role of Jesus as the advocate, the Righteous One, and the atoning sacrifice.

one who speaks ... in our defense. Since people have no basis on which to ask for forgiveness, Jesus does so on their behalf.

Righteous One. Jesus is righteous, both in the sense of being an example to follow and, especially, in the sense of not being contaminated by personal sin.

2:2 the atoning sacrifice. Jesus, the Advocate, bases his plea (that their sin should be forgiven) on the fact of his death to pay for their sin. Such a sacrifice is effective because he himself was without sin, and so could take the place of another.

17

3 Walking in Love—1 John 2:3–11

THREE-PART AGENDA

ICE-BREAKER
15 Minutes

BIBLE STUDY
30 Minutes

CARING TIME
15–45 Minutes

 LEADER: Remember to choose an appropriate ice-breaker if you have a new person at the meeting (see page M7 in the center section), and then begin with a prayer. If you have more than seven in your group, divide into groups of four for the Bible Study (see the box about the "Fearless Foursome" on page 4).

TO BEGIN THE BIBLE STUDY TIME
(Choose 1 or 2)

1. When was a time you suddenly found yourself in darkness?

2. As a child, what rule did your parents have that you broke most often (e.g., bedtime, curfew, getting homework done, etc.)?

3. Share a "hidden" talent or an unknown fact about yourself to help others in the group get to know you.

READ SCRIPTURE & DISCUSS
(If you don't have time for all the questions in this section, conclude the Bible Study [30 min.] by answering question #7.)

1. Who do you admire for the way they show love to others?

2. From this passage, what traits can you identify that mark the life of one who knows him and walks in the light?

3. What is the relationship between God's love and our obedience?

4. What is the difference between the old command and the new command (see notes on v. 7 and v. 8)?

³We know that we have come to know him if we obey his commands. ⁴The man who says, "I know him," but does not do what he commands is a liar, and the truth is not in him. ⁵But if anyone obeys his word, God's love[a] *is truly made complete in him. This is how we know we are in him: ⁶Whoever claims to live in him must walk as Jesus did.*

⁷Dear friends, I am not writing you a new command but an old one, which you have had since the beginning. This old command is the message you have heard. ⁸Yet I am writing you a new command; its truth is seen in him and you, because the darkness is passing and the true light is already shining.

⁹Anyone who claims to be in the light but hates his brother is still in the darkness. ¹⁰Whoever loves his brother lives in the light, and there is nothing in him[b] *to make him stumble. ¹¹But whoever hates his brother is in the darkness and walks around in the darkness; he does not know where he is going, because the darkness has blinded him.*

[a]5 Or *word, love for God*   [b]10 Or *it*

5. What are the characteristics of a person who walks "around in the darkness" (v. 11)? What are the consequences of living in darkness?

6. Looking over the last week, what grade would you give yourself for obeying God? What grade would you give yourself for loving others?

7. If you were hooked up to a "truth detector" right now and asked, "How are you doing, *really*?" what would you say?

CARING TIME

(Choose 1 or 2 of these questions before closing in prayer. Be sure to pray for the empty chair.)

1. How would you describe your relationship with God right now: Close? Distant? Improving? Strained? Other?

2. Does everyone in the group have a position on the team roster (review p. M5)?

3. How can the group help you in prayer this week?

Summary. John now shifts his focus. He had been addressing the secessionists by way of refuting their false claims. Now he addresses his own flock, exhorting them to follow God's commands. He does, however, point out several additional false claims (see vv. 4,6,9) within the context of his discussion of the commandment to love. Within this unit John identifies two "tests" by which people can be certain they actually know God: the test of obedience and the test of love. Those who truly know God live in his way and love as Jesus loved.

2:3–6 Thus far John has presented two truths about God which lie at the heart of the apostolic proclamation and by which the accuracy of ideas and actions are to be judged and tested. These are, first, the "... historical manifestation of the Eternal and secondly ... the fact that God is light. ... All Christian profession may be judged in relation to these truths. No thought or action can be condoned which is inconsistent either with God's nature as pure, self-giving, or with His historical palpable self-disclosure in Christ. ... This general introduction ... is now particularized in three tests—moral (the test of obedience), social (the test of love) and doctrinal (the test of belief in Christ)" (Stott). The first application of the moral test is here in verses 3–6.

2:3 We know. The New English Bible translates this opening phrase: "Here is the test by which we can make sure we know him ... ."

have come to know him. Previously John has spoken about *having fellowship with God* (see 1:3,6,7). Now he speaks about the parallel concept, that of *knowing God* (see 2:4,13–14; 3:6,16; 4:16). The verb tense indicates that he is thinking about a past experience ("we have come to know him").

if we obey his commands. The first test as to whether a person knows God, therefore, is moral in nature: does that person keep God's commands? To know God is to live in his way. The secessionists claim to know God but, as John will show, they live in a way that belies that claim.

commands. The nature of these commands is not spelled out, but the context (vv. 7–11) indicates that John probably had in mind the "great commandment" to love God and love others (Mark 12:29–31). Whatever their specific definition may be, these commands are not some external semi-arbitrary set

of rules which must be obeyed simply because they exist. These commands describe the way Jesus lived (see 2:6). They are the very pattern of the Life that John is talking about. They are what love looks like in a person's life. Unless the commands are seen in this way they will degenerate into dead ethical propositions.

> *When people live in the light, they can see where they are going. But those who reject God's viewpoint simply stumble blindly through life, bumping into all sorts of things, hurting others and hurting themselves.*

2:4 The man who says. John identifies another false claim. Those who assert that they really "know God" and yet do not keep his commandments are, in fact, lying. Such a man demonstrates by what he does that what he says is false.

does not do. The emphasis here is on sins of omission (not doing) in contrast to 1:6, where the emphasis is on sins of commission (walking in darkness).

2:5 God's love. This is the reward for obedience. God's love reaches its fulfillment in that person's life.

made complete. The verb which John uses here means ongoing fulfillment rather than static termination.

2:6 Here John introduces the idea of the "imitation of Christ." Christians are habitually to live the way Jesus lived. He is their model. As he walked, so should they walk.

live in him. This is the third phrase which John uses to describe union with God. (In 1:3 he spoke about having "fellowship" with God, and in 2:3 he spoke about "knowing" God.) To "exist in" God or to "abide in" him "suggests an intensely personal knowledge of God; it presupposes an intimate and committed relationship with him, through Jesus, which is both permanent and continuous" (Smalley).

2:7–11 If the first test of whether one is actually a Christian is moral in nature (Do you obey God?), then the second test (given here) is relational in orientation (Do you love others?).

2:7 *Dear friends.* This is literally "beloved," and is derived from the word "love" (*agape*) which is John's focus in this section.

I am not writing you a new command. This is not a new commandment because Jesus himself had stated it some years earlier and the Johannine Christians themselves had been taught it right from the beginning of their Christian walk. It is also not new in that when Jesus gave this command he was, in fact, quoting the Old Testament. He combined Leviticus 19:18 and Deuteronomy 6:5 to form the "great commandment."

command. John switches from the plural in verse 3 to the singular here since all commands are, in fact, summed up in the one great commandment (John 13:34).

2:8 *Yet I am writing you a new command.* The commandment is new in the sense that Jesus tied together two previously separate commands (that of loving God and loving others) and broadened their application. (Christians are to love everyone, not just those in their own group as shown in the parable of the Good Samaritan in Luke 10:30–37.)

its truth is seen in him and you. It is also new in that it was only in recent years that the commandment was actually lived out by Jesus and his followers. In them one saw (instead of just read about) this new kind of love (see John 10:14–18; 15:9–17).

true light. This is genuine light, in contrast to the false "light" claimed by the secessionists. This is "true light" because what it appears to be is what it actually is. Nothing is hidden. Nothing is dark.

2:9–10 John here links sets of contrasting images: light and darkness with love and hate. Those who are in the light, love. Those who are in the darkness, hate. In other words, enlightenment goes hand in hand with active care for others.

2:9 *claims.* Another false claim—that a person can actually be in God's light and yet hate others.

brother. John's primary focus here is on love and hate within the Christian community. However, the relationships between people in the church ought to be a model for all relationships.

2:10 *loves.* The Greek word John uses here is *agape*. In Greek, there are several words that can be translated by the English word "love." There is one word for sexual attraction or sexual desire (*eros*); another for family love, affection and friendship (*philia*). In contrast, *agape* refers to self-giving sacrificial action done on behalf of another who is in need, regardless of what it might cost ("Greater love has no one than this, that he lay down his life for his friends"—John 15:13), or what is felt about that other person ("Love your enemies"—Luke 6:27).

stumble. This word refers to a "trap" or a "snare" that causes one to fall into sin or error.

2:11 *hates.* If a person does not love, that is, does not care for the needs of another in direct, active ways, then such a person hates. It is either love or hate in John's view. He does not offer neutrality as a comfortable third option in relationships. In the same way John describes love in terms of deeds, not feelings, so too "hate" has little to do with feelings of hostility toward others. "Hate" is the lack of loving deeds done on their behalf.

walks around in the darkness. When people live in the light, they can see where they are going. But those who reject God's viewpoint simply stumble blindly through life, bumping into all sorts of things, hurting others and hurting themselves.

> *If a person does not love, that is, does not care for the needs of another in direct, active ways, then such a person hates.*

blinded. Living apart from God's way (i.e., "in darkness") will yield over time moral and spiritual blindness so that it becomes more and more difficult for one to see what is and is not true or good. Hatred distorts perception.

4 Stages of Faith—1 John 2:12–17

THREE-PART AGENDA

ICE-BREAKER
15 Minutes

BIBLE STUDY
30 Minutes

CARING TIME
15–45 Minutes

 LEADER: If there's a new person in this session, start with an ice-breaker from the center section (see page M7). Remember to stick closely to the three-part agenda and the time allowed for each segment. Is your group praying for the empty chair? As the leader, you may want to choose question #1 in the Caring Time to facilitate the group in handling accountability issues.

TO BEGIN THE BIBLE STUDY TIME
(Choose 1 or 2)

1. What do you love the most about the area in which you live?

2. How are you at answering your mail / e-mail?

3. Growing up, what habit did you have that really annoyed your parents?

READ SCRIPTURE & DISCUSS
(If you don't have time for all the questions in this section, conclude the Bible Study [30 min.] by answering question #7.)

1. Who encourages you to "hang in there" when the going gets tough?

2. In your spiritual life, which of the three stages John addresses in verses 12–14 can you most relate to: "Children"—just beginning? "Young men"—at the peak of their strength? "Fathers"—seasoned veterans?

¹²I write to you, dear children,
   because your sins have been forgiven on
      account of his name.
¹³I write to you, fathers,
   because you have known him who is from
      the beginning.
I write to you, young men,
   because you have overcome the evil one.
I write to you, dear children,
   because you have known the Father.
¹⁴I write to you, fathers,
   because you have known him who is from
      the beginning.
I write to you, young men,
   because you are strong,
   and the word of God lives in you,
   and you have overcome the evil one.

Do Not Love the World

¹⁵Do not love the world or anything in the world. If any-one loves the world, the love of the Father is not in him. ¹⁶For everything in the world—the cravings of sinful man, the lust of his eyes and the boasting of what he has and does—comes not from the Father but from the world. ¹⁷The world and its desires pass away, but the man who does the will of God lives forever.

3. How is John affirming these Christians in their faith? Which of the reminders in these verses do you most need to hear?

4. What does John mean by "the world" (vv. 15–17)? What does it mean to love the world? What happens to the person who loves the world more than God?

5. What two options does a person have, and what is the end result of each option (v. 17)?

6. On a scale of 1 (a little) to 10 (a lot), how attached to the world do you feel? How does that compare to a year ago?

7. In what way can you show more devotion and commitment to God?

CARING TIME

(Choose 1 or 2 of these questions before closing in prayer. Be sure to pray for the empty chair.)

1. For what would you like this group to help hold you accountable?

2. How are you doing at inviting others to the group? Who could you invite for next week?

3. How can the group support you in prayer this week?

Summary. In contrast to those who walk in darkness—and about whom John has just been writing (2:9–11)—he now turns to those who are committed to the light. He has two things to say to the Christian community. First, he assures them of their standing before God (vv. 12–14); and second, he warns them about loving the world (vv. 15–17). It is worth noting that up to this point in his epistle John has always led off his argument by first stating false claims, but here his focus is on true claims.

2:12–14 In six parallel and almost poetic statements John addresses three groups of Christians by using the terminology of a family. It is not completely clear to whom John is referring with the titles "children," "fathers," and "young men." In fact, he may not have actual groups in mind and is simply thinking about different stages of the spiritual life (the innocence of childhood, the strength of youth, and the mature knowledge of age, as Augustine put it). Some scholars feel that John is addressing the whole community by means of the term "dear children," much as

> *To give oneself over to the love of the world is foolish because the world with its values and goods is already passing away. Those who love the world will pass away with it, while those who love God will live forever.*

the wisdom teachers of the Old Testament addressed their followers. He then speaks to two groups of believers within the community of "dear children": those who have been Christians for a long time (the fathers) and those who are newer members of the faith (the young men).

2:12 children. John affirms two foundational truths: they are forgiven (v. 12) and they do know God (v. 13c). It is important that the Christians in John's church be assured this is true for them. The secessionists are claiming that they have experienced forgiveness and that they know God, but John has rejected their claims (1:6–10; 2:4). Lest his own flock fear their claims to such reality are also being rejected, John assures them that they are in a dif-

ferent place from the secessionists. Here he reaffirms that the walk of faith begins with these two experiences.

have been forgiven. The verb tense indicates that John is thinking of the forgiveness that comes at the time of conversion, whereas in 1:9 his concern was with ongoing forgiveness for subsequent sins based on the confession of sins.

name. In the Near East a name is very significant. It is not just a convenient word for distinguishing one person from another. It is a description of the essential character of that person. Thus, the name Jesus recalls not just who he is but his atoning work through which forgiveness has been made possible (1:7; 2:1–2).

2:13 fathers. "[These are the] spiritually adult in the congregation. Their first flash of ecstasy in receiving forgiveness and fellowship with the Father was an experience of long ago. Even the battles of the young man, to which he will next refer, are past. The fathers have progressed into a deep communion with God" (Stott).

you have known him. The message to the "fathers" here and in verse 14 is identical. John reassures them that they do, indeed, know Christ. Once again, John uses the perfect tense for the verb. In this way he emphasizes the present consequences of a past event. This same tense is used for each of the main verbs in the six messages.

him who is from the beginning. The reference is probably to Jesus since it echoes the phrase by which John opens his letter: "that which was from the beginning" which is a direct reference to Jesus.

young men. John asserts that the Christian life involves spiritual warfare. To be a Christian does not merely entail the enjoyment of sins forgiven and a warm relationship with God. It is also a vigorous battle against evil.

overcome. "Overcoming" is an important theme in all of John's writing (see John 16:33; 1 John 4:4; 5:4–5; Rev. 2:7ff). In the same way that Christ overcame Satan via his death and resurrection, so too Christians are to overcome the evil one. Twice the "young men" are commended for showing themselves to be spiritually strong enough to have overcome Satan (vv. 13–14).

the evil one. Satan, the ruler of darkness (see vv. 8–11) and the source of evil.

children. In Greek, a different word is used here for "children" than is used in verse 12. In verse 12 the word is *tekna* and emphasizes the kinship that exists between children and parents. Here, the word is *paidia*. It emphasizes the age of children, i.e., they are young and in need of training. However, these distinctions are minor and are more ones of nuance than substance.

because you have known the Father. Not only do Christians experience the forgiveness of sins (see v. 12a), they also enter into a personal relationship with God.

2:14 word of God. This is the source of the overcoming power displayed by the "young men." They know God's will and have lived in conformity to it.

lives in you. The word of God is meant not only to be understood, but it is also intended to be incorporated into a person's very being.

2:15–17 Having just assured his hearers about their secure relationship with God, John now finds it necessary to warn them about an attitude that could bring them down, lest they now feel immune to the power of evil. The attitude they are to avoid is "love of the world." John bases his command on two factors: the incompatibility of love for God with love for the world (vv. 15–16), and the transience of worldly desires in comparison to the everlasting life of those who do God's will (v. 17). John is attacking an attitude (love of the world). He is not attacking "things" *per se*, much less people.

2:15 love. As in verse 5 and verse 10, the love which John speaks about is not so much an emotional response as it is the act of caring, expressed by what a person does. As such, this "love" is appropriately directed toward God (v. 5) and toward others (v. 10), but not toward the pleasures of the world.

world. The word John uses here is *kosmos* and in this context it means that which is alienated from God and is, in fact, contrary to who God is. It refers to pagan culture which has abandoned God. "Our author means human society insofar as it is organized on wrong principles and characterized by base desires, false values and egoism" (Dodd).

2:16 everything. Since God created the world (John 1:3), John cannot mean that everything in the world is automatically evil. In this verse, it is evident that what he had in mind are those aspects of the world which stand in opposition to God's ways.

cravings. That part of human nature which demands gratification—be it for sexual pleasure, for luxury, for possessions, for expensive food, for whatever.

lust of his eyes. Greed which is aroused by sight. A person sees something and wants it. (For examples of this, see Gen. 3:6; Josh. 7:21; 2 Sam. 11:2–4.)

boasting. Pride in one's possessions; an attitude of arrogance because one has acquired so much. In its original Greek usage, this word referred to a man who claimed to be important because he had achieved so much when, in fact, he really had done very little. These three attitudes are interconnected. "Selfish human desire is stimulated by what the eye sees and expresses itself in outward show" (Marshall). Taken together they add up to a materialistic view of the world.

> *The word of God is meant not only to be understood, but it is also intended to be incorporated into a person's very being.*

2:17 pass away. To give oneself over to the love of the world is foolish because the world with its values and goods is already passing away (v. 8). Those who love the world will pass away with it, while those who love God will live forever.

lives forever. In contrast to those who live for the moment are those who give themselves to eternal, unchanging realities. Eternal life is one of God's gifts to the Christian.

5 Antichrists—1 John 2:18–27

THREE-PART AGENDA

ICE-BREAKER
15 Minutes

BIBLE STUDY
30 Minutes

CARING TIME
15–45 Minutes

LEADER: Check page M7 in the center section for a good ice-breaker, particularly if you have a new person at this meeting. Is your group working well together—with everyone "fielding their position" as shown on the team roster on page M5?

TO BEGIN THE BIBLE STUDY TIME
(Choose 1 or 2)

1. What did you do the hour right before coming to this study?

2. Growing up, what "crowd" or person did your parents warn you to stay away from?

3. How can you tell when someone is not telling you the truth?

READ SCRIPTURE & DISCUSS
(If you don't have time for all the questions in this section, conclude the Bible Study [30 min.] by answering question #7.)

1. If you only had one hour left to live, how would you spend this time?

2. What made John feel he was in "the last hour" (see note on v. 18)?

3. John says, "even now many antichrists have come" (v. 18). Who do you think he had in mind? What comes to your mind when you hear the word "antichrist"?

4. What standard should we use to evaluate the truth of what someone is teaching?

Warning Against Antichrists

[18]*Dear children, this is the last hour; and as you have heard that the antichrist is coming, even now many antichrists have come. This is how we know it is the last hour.* [19]*They went out from us, but they did not really belong to us. For if they had belonged to us, they would have remained with us; but their going showed that none of them belonged to us.*

[20]*But you have an anointing from the Holy One, and all of you know the truth.*[a] [21]*I do not write to you because you do not know the truth, but because you do know it and because no lie comes from the truth.* [22]*Who is the liar? It is the man who denies that Jesus is the Christ. Such a man is the antichrist—he denies the Father and the Son.* [23]*No one who denies the Son has the Father; whoever acknowledges the Son has the Father also.*

[24]*See that what you have heard from the beginning remains in you. If it does, you also will remain in the Son and in the Father.* [25]*And this is what he promised us—even eternal life.*

[26]*I am writing these things to you about those who are trying to lead you astray.* [27]*As for you, the anointing you received from him remains in you, and you do not need anyone to teach you. But as his anointing teaches you about all things and as that anointing is real, not counterfeit—just as it has taught you, remain in him.*

[a]20 Some manuscripts *and you know all things*

5. What is promised to those who remain steadfast in the truth? How does that promise encourage you today?

6. Where do you need "the anointing" (v. 27) of the Holy Spirit in your life? What would you like the Holy Spirit to teach you?

7. What can help you "remain in him" (v. 27) in the coming week?

CARING TIME

(Choose 1 or 2 of these questions before closing in prayer. Be sure to pray for the empty chair.)

1. How is the group doing with its "team assignments" (review the roster on p. M5)?

2. What is something for which you are particularly thankful?

3. How can this group remember you in prayer this week?

Summary. Having assured the members of his church that they are walking in the Christian way, John returns to the question of how to distinguish between those who are true Christians and those who are counterfeit Christians. Thus far in his epistle he has defined two tests which enable one to make such a distinction: the true Christian is obedient to God's commands (the moral test, 2:3–6) and the true Christian loves other people (the social test, 2:7–11). Now he adds a third test: the true Christian remains firmly committed to the truth of God. This is the doctrinal test (Stott).

2:18 the last hour. The early Christians understood clearly that the first coming of Christ (the Incarnation) inaugurated "the last days." They also knew that his second coming (the *parousia*) would bring to a close the "last days" and usher in a new age in which God's rule would be visible and universal. In the first century the expectation was that this second coming of Jesus would take place in the immediate future. It could, in fact, happen at literally any moment. In this passage, one catches this sense of urgency. "The time is short," John is saying, "this is the last hour. He is coming back. So be ready." It is almost as if a clock is ticking away the final moments before the Second Coming.

antichrist. Although John is the only New Testament writer to use this term (see 2:22; 4:3; 2 John 7), the same concept is present in other parts of Scripture (e.g., Mark 13:22 and 2 Thess. 2:1–12), namely that one day an opponent to Christ will arise who is the incarnation of evil and Satan—just as Christ was the incarnation of good and God.

antichrists. John points out that the coming of the Antichrist was not just some future threat. Even at that moment the "spirit of the antichrist" (see 4:3) was loose in the world and active in those who deny Christ and his teachings (see v. 22).

2:19 They went out from us. John now identifies those who are imbued with the spirit of the antichrist. They are none other than the secessionists who left the church and even now seek to win over their former friends and colleagues to their point of view (see v. 26).

2:20 an anointing. In the Old Testament, when a king or a priest was consecrated to God's service,

oil was poured on them as part of the ceremony. Here the noun refers to the *means* of anointing, namely the Holy Spirit. Just as Jesus was anointed with the Holy Spirit (Luke 4:18; Acts 10:38), so too is the believer. The Holy Spirit is thus the one that guides the Christian into all truth (John 14:17; 15:26; 16:13).

all of you. In contrast to the secessionists who claimed to have special, esoteric insight into spiritual truth not available to others (this was the source of their new doctrine), John assures his readers that *all* Christians know the truth, not just an elite few.

> John's reasoning is this: true Christians have the Holy Spirit and therefore know the truth. Those who know the truth do not lie (which is what he says here). Therefore, the implication is that those who are lying by teaching false doctrines do not know the truth because they do not have the Holy Spirit and thus they are not true Christians.

know the truth. The departure of the secessionists from the church was not the only evidence that "they did not really belong to us." The Christians already knew that they espoused false doctrines by virtue of their Holy Spirit derived insight into what was true.

2:21 no lie comes from the truth. John's reasoning is this: true Christians have the Holy Spirit and therefore know the truth (v. 20). Those who know the truth do not lie (which is what he says here). Therefore, the implication is that those who are lying by teaching false doctrines do not know the truth because they do not have the Holy Spirit and thus they are not true Christians.

2:22 John now reveals the master lie in the secessionists' false teaching; they deny that Jesus is the Messiah and the Son of God. This is an obvious lie that all true Christians will immediately recognize. "The antichrists probably taught (as some later Gnostics certainly taught) that Jesus was born and

Leadership Training Supplement

YOU ARE HERE

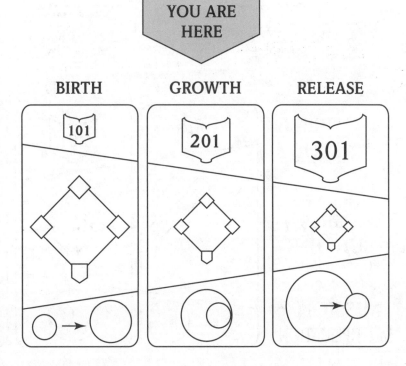

BIRTH   GROWTH   RELEASE

101   201   301

What is the game plan for your group in the 201 stage?

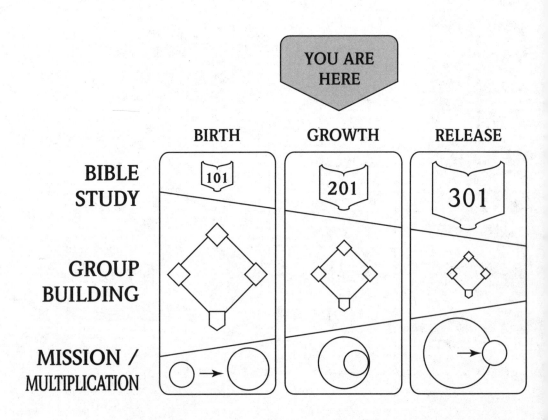

YOU ARE HERE

	BIRTH	GROWTH	RELEASE
BIBLE STUDY	101	201	301
GROUP BUILDING			
MISSION / MULTIPLICATION			

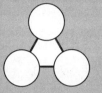

The 3-Legged Stool

The three essentials in a healthy small group are Bible Study, Group Building and Mission / Multiplication. You need all three to stay balanced—like a 3-legged stool.

- To focus only on Bible Study will lead to scholasticism.
- To focus only on Group Building will lead to narcissism.
- To focus only on Mission will lead to burnout.

You need a game plan for the life cycle of the group where all of these elements are present in a purpose-driven strategy:

Bible Study

To dig into Scripture as a group.

Group Bible Study is quite different from individual Bible Study. The guided discussion questions are open-ended. And for those with little Bible background, there are reference notes to bring this person up to speed.

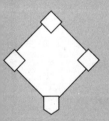

Group Building

To transform your group into a mission-driven team.

The nine basic needs of a group will be assigned to nine different people. Everyone has a job to fill, and when everyone is doing their job the group will grow spiritually and numerically. When new people enter the group, there is a selection of ICE-BREAKERS to start off the meeting and let the new people get acquainted.

Mission / Multiplication

To identify the Apprentice / Leader for birthing a new group.

In this stage, you will start dreaming about the possibility of starting a new group down the road. The questions at the close of each session will lead you carefully through the dreaming process—to help you discover an Apprentice / Leader who will eventually be the leader of a new group. This is an exciting challenge! (See page M6 for more about Mission / Multiplication.)

Bible Study

What is unique about Serendipity Group Bible Study?

Bible Study for groups is based on six principles. Principle 1: Level the playing field so that everyone can share—those who know the Bible and those who do not know the Bible. Principle 2: Share your spiritual story and let the people in your group get to know you. Principle 3: Ask open-ended questions that have no right or wrong answers. Principle 4: Keep a tight agenda. Principle 5: Subdivide into smaller groups so that everyone can participate. Principle 6: Affirm One Another—"Thanks for sharing."

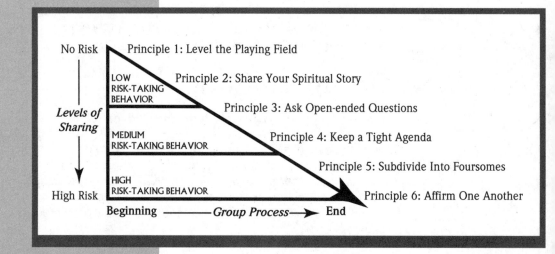

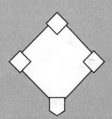

Group Building

What are the jobs that are needed on your team roster?

In the first or second session of this course, you need to fill out the roster on the next page. Then check every few weeks to see that everyone is "playing their position." If you do not have nine people in your group, you can double up on jobs until new people join your group and are assigned a job.

Your Small Group Team Roster

Mission Leader
(Left Field)
Keeps group focused on the mission to invite new people and eventually give birth to a new group. This person needs to be passionate and have a long-term perspective.

_____

Host
(Center Field)
Environmental engineer in charge of meeting location. Always on the lookout for moving to a new meeting location where new people will feel the "home field advantage."

_____

Social Leader
(Right Field)
Designates who is going to bring refreshments. Plans a party every month or so where new people are invited to visit and children are welcome.

_____

Caretaker
(Shortstop)
Takes new members under their wing. Makes sure they get acquainted. Always has an extra book, name tags and a list of group members and phone numbers.

_____

Bible Study Leader
(Second Base)
Takes over in the Bible Study time (30 minutes). Follows the agenda. Keeps the group moving. This person must be very time-conscious.

_____

Group Leader
(Pitcher)
Puts ball in play. Team encourager. Motivator. Sees to it that everyone is involved in the team effort.

_____

Caring Time Leader
(Third Base)
Takes over in the Caring Time. Records prayer requests and follows up on any prayer needs during the week. This person is the "heart" of the group.

_____

Worship Leader
(First Base)
Starts the meeting with singing and prayer. If a new person comes, shifts immediately to an ice-breaker to get acquainted, before the opening prayer.

_____

Apprentice / Leader
(Catcher)
The other half of the battery. Observes the infield. Calls "time" to discuss strategy and regroup. Stays focused.

_____

Mission / Multiplication

Where are you in the 3-stage life cycle of your mission?

You can't sit on a one-legged stool—or even a two-legged stool. It takes all three. The same is true of a small group; you need all three legs. A Bible Study and Care Group will eventually fall if it does not have a mission.

The mission goal is to eventually give birth to a new group. In this 201 course, the goals are: 1) to keep inviting new people to join your group and 2) to discover the Apprentice / Leader and leadership core for starting a new group down the road.

When a new person comes to the group, start off the meeting with one of the ice-breakers on the following pages. These ice-breakers are designed to be fun and easy to share, but they have a very important purpose—that is, to let the new person get acquainted with the group and share their spiritual story with the group, and hear the spiritual stories of those in the group.

YOU ARE HERE

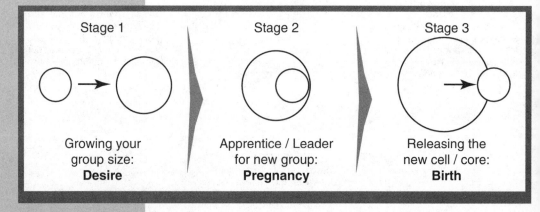

Stage 1	Stage 2	Stage 3
Growing your group size: **Desire**	Apprentice / Leader for new group: **Pregnancy**	Releasing the new cell / core: **Birth**

Ice-Breakers

I Am Somebody Who ...

Rotate around the group, one person reading the first item, the next person reading the second item, etc. Before answering, let everyone in the group try to GUESS what the answer would be: "Yes" ... "No" ... or "Maybe." After everyone has guessed, explain the answer. Anyone who guessed right gets $10. When every item on the list has been read, the person with the most "money" WINS.

I AM SOMEBODY WHO ...

Y	N	M		Y	N	M	
❑	❑	❑	would go on a blind date	❑	❑	❑	would enjoy skydiving
❑	❑	❑	sings in the shower	❑	❑	❑	has a black belt in karate
❑	❑	❑	listens to music full blast	❑	❑	❑	watches soap operas
❑	❑	❑	likes to dance	❑	❑	❑	is afraid of the dark
❑	❑	❑	cries at movies	❑	❑	❑	goes to bed early
❑	❑	❑	stops to smell the flowers	❑	❑	❑	plays the guitar
❑	❑	❑	daydreams a lot	❑	❑	❑	talks to plants
❑	❑	❑	likes to play practical jokes	❑	❑	❑	will ask a stranger for directions
❑	❑	❑	makes a "to do" list	❑	❑	❑	sleeps until the last second
❑	❑	❑	loves liver	❑	❑	❑	likes to travel alone
❑	❑	❑	won't use a portable toilet	❑	❑	❑	reads the financial page
❑	❑	❑	likes thunderstorms	❑	❑	❑	saves for a rainy day
❑	❑	❑	enjoys romance novels	❑	❑	❑	lies about my age
❑	❑	❑	loves crossword puzzles	❑	❑	❑	yells at the umpire
❑	❑	❑	hates flying	❑	❑	❑	closes my eyes during scary movies
❑	❑	❑	fixes my own car				

Press Conference

This is a great activity for a new group or when new people are joining an established group. Interview one person with these questions.

1. What is your nickname and how did you get it?

2. Where did you grow up? Where was the "watering hole" in your hometown—where kids got together?

3. What did you do for kicks then? What about now?

4. What was the turning point in your spiritual life?

5. What prompted you to come to this group?

6. What do you want to get out of this group?

Down Memory Lane

Celebrate the childhood memories of the way you were. Choose one or more of the topics listed below and take turns answering the question related to it. If time allows, do another round.

HOME SWEET HOME–What do you remember about your childhood home?

TELEVISION—What was your favorite TV program or radio show?

OLD SCHOOLHOUSE—What were your best and worst subjects in school?

LIBRARY—What did you like to read (and where)?

TELEPHONE—How much time did you spend on the phone each day?

MOVIES—Who was your favorite movie star?

CASH FLOW—What did you do for spending money?

SPORTS—What was your favorite sport or team?

GRANDPA'S HOUSE—Where did your grandparents live? When did you visit them?

POLICE—Did you ever get in trouble with the law?

WEEKENDS—What was the thing to do on Saturday night?

Wallet Scavenger Hunt

With your wallet or purse, use the set of questions below. You get two minutes in silence to go through your possessions and find these items. Then break the silence and "show-and-tell" what you have chosen. For instance, "The thing I have had for the longest time is ... this picture of me when I was a baby."

1. The thing I have had for the LONGEST TIME in my wallet is ...

2. The thing that has SENTIMENTAL VALUE is ...

3. The thing that reminds me of a FUN TIME is ...

4. The most REVEALING thing about me in my wallet is ...

The Grand Total

This is a fun ice-breaker that has additional uses. You can use this ice-breaker to divide your group into two subgroups (odds and evens). You can also calculate who has the highest and lowest totals if you need a fun way to select someone to do a particular task, such as bring refreshments or be first to tell their story.

Fill each box with the correct number and then total your score. When everyone is finished, go around the group and explain how you got your total.

☐ X	☐ =	☐
Number of hours you sleep	Number of miles you walk daily	Subtotal
☐ −	☐ =	☐
Number of speeding tickets you've received	Number of times sent to principal's office	Subtotal
☐ ÷	☐ =	☐
Number of hours spent watching TV daily	Number of books you read this year for fun	Subtotal
☐ +	☐ =	☐
Number of push-ups you can do	Number of pounds you lost this year	Subtotal

☐

GRAND
TOTAL

Find Yourself in the Picture

In this drawing, which child do you identify with—or which one best portrays you right now? Share with your group which child you would choose and why. You can also use this as an affirmation exercise, by assigning each person in your group to a child in the picture.

Four Facts, One Lie

Everyone in the group should answer the following five questions. One of the five answers should be a lie! The rest of the group members can guess which of your answers is a lie.

1. At age 7, my favorite TV show was ...

2. At age 9, my hero was ...

3. At age 11, I wanted to be a ...

4. At age 13, my favorite music was ...

5. Right now, my favorite pastime is ...

Old-Fashioned Auction

Just like an old-fashioned auction, conduct an out loud auction in your group—starting each item at $50. Everybody starts out with $1,000. Select an auctioneer. This person can also get in on the bidding. Remember, start the bidding on each item at $50. Then, write the winning bid in the left column and the winner's name in the right column. Remember, you only have $1,000 to spend for the whole game. AUCTIONEER: Start off by asking, "Who will give me $50 for a 1965 red MG convertible?" ... and keep going until you have a winner. Keep this auction to 10 minutes.

WINNING BID   WINNER

$_____ 1965 red MG convertible in perfect condition   _____

$_____ Winter vacation in Hawaii for two   _____

$_____ Two Super Bowl tickets on the 50-yard line   _____

$_____ One year of no hassles with my kids / parents   _____

$_____ Holy Land tour hosted by my favorite Christian   _____
                leader

$_____ Season pass to ski resort of my choice   _____

$_____ Two months off to do anything I want, with pay   _____

$_____ Home theater with surround sound   _____

$_____ Breakfast in bed for one year   _____

$_____ Two front-row tickets at the concert of my choice   _____

$_____ Two-week Caribbean cruise with my spouse in   _____
                honeymoon suite

$_____ Shopping spree at Saks Fifth Avenue   _____

$_____ Six months of maid service   _____

$_____ All-expense-paid family vacation to Disney World   _____

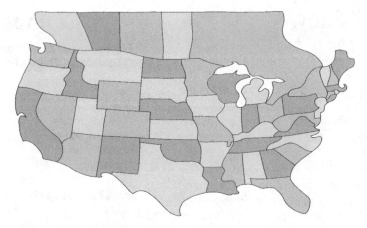

Places in My Life

On the map above, put six dots to indicate these significant places in your journey. Then go around and have each person explain the dots:

- the place where I was born
- the place where I spent most of my life
- the place where I first fell in love
- the place where I went or would like to go on a honeymoon
- the place where God first became real to me
- the place where I would like to retire

The Four Quaker Questions

This is an old Quaker activity which Serendipity has adapted over the years. Go around the group and share your answers to the questions, everyone answering #1. Then, everyone answers #2, etc. This ice-breaker has been known to take between 30 and 60 minutes for some groups.

1. Where were you living between the ages of 7 and 12, and what were the winters like then?

2. How was your home heated during that time?

3. What was the center of warmth in your life when you were a child? (It could be a place in the house, a time of year, a person, etc.)

4. When did God become a "warm" person to you ... and how did it happen?

KWIZ Show

Like a TV quiz show, someone from the group picks a category and reads the four questions—pausing to let the others in the group guess before revealing the answer. When the first person is finished, everyone adds up the money they won by guessing right. Go around the group and have each person take a category. The person with the most money at the end wins. To begin, ask one person to choose a CATEGORY and read out loud the $1 question. Before answering, let everyone try to GUESS the answer. When everyone has guessed, the person answers the question, and anyone who guessed right puts $1 in the margin, etc. until the first person has read all four questions in the CATEGORY.

Clothes

For $1: I'm more likely to shop at:
❐ Sears ❐ Saks Fifth Avenue

For $2: I feel more comfortable wearing:
❐ formal clothes
❐ casual clothes
❐ sport clothes
❐ grubbies

For $3: In buying clothes, I look for:
❐ fashion / style
❐ price
❐ name brand
❐ quality

For $4: In buying clothes, I usually:
❐ shop all day for a bargain
❐ go to one store, but try on everything
❐ buy the first thing I try on
❐ buy without trying it on

Tastes

For $1: In music, I am closer to:
❐ Bach ❐ Beatles

For $2: In furniture, I prefer:
❐ Early American
❐ French Provincial
❐ Scandinavian—contemporary
❐ Hodgepodge—little of everything

For $3: My favorite choice of reading material is:
❐ science fiction ❐ sports
❐ mystery ❐ romance

For $4: If I had $1,000 to splurge, I would buy:
❐ one original painting
❐ two numbered prints
❐ three reproductions and an easy chair
❐ four cheap imitations, an easy chair and a color TV

Travel

For $1: For travel, I prefer:
❐ excitement ❐ enrichment

For $2: On a vacation, my lifestyle is:
❐ go-go all the time
❐ slow and easy
❐ party every night and sleep in

For $3: In packing for a trip, I include:
❐ toothbrush and change of underwear
❐ light bag and good book
❐ small suitcase and nice outfit
❐ all but the kitchen sink

For $4: If I had money to blow, I would choose:
❐ one glorious night in a luxury hotel
❐ a weekend in a nice hotel
❐ a full week in a cheap motel
❐ two weeks camping in the boondocks

Habits

For $1: I am more likely to squeeze the toothpaste:
☐ in the middle ☐ from the end

For $2: If I am lost, I will probably:
☐ stop and ask directions
☐ check the map
☐ find the way by driving around

For $3: I read the newspaper starting with the:
☐ front page
☐ funnies
☐ sports
☐ entertainment section

For $4: When I get ready for bed, I put my clothes:
☐ on a hanger in the closet
☐ folded neatly over a chair
☐ into a hamper or clothes basket
☐ on the floor

Shows

For $1: I am more likely to:
☐ go see a first-run movie
☐ rent a video at home

For $2: On TV, my first choice is:
☐ news
☐ sports
☐ sitcoms

For $3: If a show gets too scary, I will usually:
☐ go to the restroom
☐ close my eyes
☐ clutch a friend
☐ love it

For $4: In movies, I prefer:
☐ romantic comedies
☐ serious drama
☐ action films
☐ Disney animation

Food

For $1: I prefer to eat at a:
☐ fast-food restaurant
☐ fancy restaurant

For $2: On the menu, I look for something:
☐ familiar
☐ different
☐ way-out

For $3: When eating chicken, my preference is a:
☐ drumstick
☐ wing
☐ breast
☐ gizzard

For $4: I draw the line when it comes to eating:
☐ frog legs
☐ snails
☐ raw oysters
☐ Rocky Mountain oysters

Work

For $1: I prefer to work at a job that is:
☐ too big to handle
☐ too small to be challenging

For $2: The job I find most unpleasant to do is:
☐ cleaning the house
☐ working in the yard
☐ balancing the checkbook

For $3: In choosing a job, I look for:
☐ salary
☐ security
☐ fulfillment
☐ working conditions

For $4: If I had to choose between these jobs, I would choose:
☐ pickle inspector at processing plant
☐ complaint officer at department store
☐ bedpan changer at hospital
☐ personnel manager in charge of firing

Let Me Tell You About My Day

What was your day like today? Use one of the characters below to help you describe your day to the group. Feel free to elaborate.

GREEK TRAGEDY
It was classic, not a dry eye
in the house.

ACTION ADVENTURE
When I rode onto the
scene, everybody noticed.

BORING LECTURE
The biggest
challenge of the day was
staying awake.

**EPISODE OF
THREE STOOGES**
I was Larry, trapped
between Curly and Moe.

BIBLE EPIC
Cecil B. DeMille couldn't
have done it any better.

SOAP OPERA
I didn't think these
things could happen,
until it happened to me.

LATE NIGHT NEWS
It might as well have
been broadcast over the
airwaves.

FIREWORKS DISPLAY
It was spectacular.

PROFESSIONAL WRESTLING MATCH
I feel as if Hulk Hogan's been coming after me.

Music in My Life

Put an *"X"* on the first line below—somewhere between the two extremes—to indicate how you are feeling right now. Share your answers, and then repeat this process down the list. If you feel comfortable, briefly explain your response.

IN MY PERSONAL LIFE, I'M FEELING LIKE ...
Blues in the Night_____ **Feeling Groovy**

IN MY FAMILY LIFE, I'M FEELING LIKE ...
Stormy Weather _____ **The Sound of Music**

IN MY EMOTIONAL LIFE, I'M FEELING LIKE ...
The Feeling Is Gone _____ **On Eagle's Wings**

IN MY WORK, SCHOOL OR CAREER, I'M FEELING LIKE ...
Take This Job and Shove It _____ **The Future's So Bright I Gotta Wear Shades**

IN MY SPIRITUAL LIFE, I'M FEELING LIKE ...
Sounds of Silence _____ **Hallelujah Chorus**

My Childhood Table

Try to recall the table where you ate most of your meals as a child, and the people who sat around that table. Use the questions below to describe these significant relationships, and how they helped to shape the person you are today.

1. What was the shape of the table?
2. Where did you sit?
3. Who else was at the table?
4. If you had to describe each person with a color, what would be the color of (for instance):
   - ❑ Your father? (e.g., dark blue, because he was conservative like IBM)
   - ❑ Your mother? (e.g., light green, because she reminded me of springtime)
5. If you had to describe the atmosphere at the table with a color, what would you choose? (e.g., bright orange, because it was warm and light)
6. Who was the person at the table who praised you and made you feel special?
7. Who provided the spiritual leadership in your home?

Home Improvement

Take inventory of your own life. Bob Munger, in his booklet *My Heart—Christ's Home*, describes the areas of a person's life as the rooms of a house. Give yourself a grade on each room as follows, then share with the others your best and worst grade.

    ❐ A = excellent   ❐ C = passing, needs a little dusting

    ❐ B = good   ❐ D = passing, but needs a lot of improvement

LIBRARY: This room is in your mind—what you allow to go into it and come out of it. It is the "control room" of the entire house.

DINING ROOM: Appetites, desires; those things your mind and spirit feed on for nourishment.

DRAWING ROOM: This is where you draw close to God—seeking time with him daily, not just in times of distress or need.

WORKSHOP: This room is where your gifts, talents and skills are put to work for God—by the power of the Spirit.

RUMPUS ROOM: The social area of your life; the things you do to amuse yourself and others.

HALL CLOSET: The one secret place that no one knows about, but is a real stumbling block in your walk in the Spirit.

How Is It With Your Soul?

John Wesley, the founder of the Methodist Church, asked his "class meetings" to check in each week at their small group meeting with this question: "How is it with your soul?" To answer this question, choose one of these four allegories to explain the past week in your life:

WEATHER: For example: "This week has been mostly cloudy, with some thunderstorms at midweek. Right now, the weather is a little brighter ..."

MUSIC: For example: "This past week has been like heavy rock music—almost too loud. The sound seems to reverberate off the walls."

COLOR: For example: "This past week has been mostly fall colors—deep orange, flaming red and pumpkin."

SEASON OF THE YEAR: For example: "This past week has been like springtime. New signs of life are beginning to appear on the barren trees, and a few shoots of winter wheat are breaking through the frozen ground."

My Spiritual Journey

The half-finished sentences below are designed to help you share your spiritual story. Ask one person to finish all the sentences. Then move to the next person, etc. If you are short on time, have only one person tell their story in this session.

1. RELIGIOUS BACKGROUND: My spiritual story begins in my home as a child, where the religious training was ...

2. CHURCH: The church that I went to as a child was ...

3. SIGNIFICANT PERSON: The person who had the greatest influence on my spiritual formation was ...

4. PERSONAL ENCOUNTER: The first time God became more than just a name to me was when ...

5. JOURNEY: Since my personal encounter with God, my Christian life might be described as ...

6. PRESENT: On a scale from 1 to 10, I would describe my spiritual energy level right now as a ...

7. NEXT STEP: The thing I need to work on right now in my spiritual life is ...

Bragging Rights

Check your group for bragging rights in these categories.

❑ SPEEDING TICKETS: the person with the most speeding tickets

❑ BROKEN BONES: the person with the most broken bones

❑ STITCHES: the person with the most stitches

❑ SCARS: the person with the longest scar

❑ FISH OR GAME: the person who claims they caught the largest fish or killed the largest animal

❑ STUNTS: the person with the most death-defying story

❑ IRON: the person who can pump the most iron

Personal Habits

Have everyone in your group finish the sentence on the first category by putting an "*X*" somewhere between the two extremes (e.g., on HOUSEWORK ... I would put myself closer to "Where's the floor?"). Repeat this process down the list as time permits.

ON HOUSEWORK, I AM SOMEWHERE BETWEEN:
Eat off the floor_____Where's the floor?

ON COOKING, I AM SOMEWHERE BETWEEN:
Every meal is an act of worship_____Make it fast and hold the frills

ON EXERCISING, I AM SOMEWHERE BETWEEN:
Workout every morning_____Click the remote

ON SHOPPING, I AM SOMEWHERE BETWEEN:
Shop all day for a bargain_____Only the best

ON EATING, I AM SOMEWHERE BETWEEN:
You are what you eat_____Eat, drink and be merry

American Graffiti

If Hollywood made a movie about your life on the night of your high school prom, what would be needed? Let each person in your group have a few minutes to recall these details. If you have more than four or five in your group, ask everyone to choose two or three topics to talk about.

1. LOCATION: Where were you living?
2. WEIGHT: How much did you weigh—soaking wet?
3. PROM: Where was it held?
4. DATE: Who did you go with?
5. CAR / TRANSPORTATION: How did you get there?
   (If you used a car, what was the model, year, color, condition?)
6. ATTIRE: What did you wear?
7. PROGRAM: What was the entertainment?
8. AFTERWARD: What did you do afterward?
9. HIGHLIGHT: What was the highlight of the evening?
10. HOMECOMING: If you could go back and visit your high school, who would you like to see?

Group Orchestra

Read out loud the first item and let everyone nominate the person in your group for this musical instrument in your group orchestra. Then, read aloud the next instrument, and call out another name, etc.

ANGELIC HARP: Soft, gentle, melodious, wooing with heavenly sounds.

OLD-FASHIONED WASHBOARD: Nonconforming, childlike and fun.

PLAYER PIANO: Mischievous, raucous, honky-tonk—delightfully carefree.

KETTLEDRUM: Strong, vibrant, commanding when needed but usually in the background.

PASSIONATE CASTANET: Full of Spanish fervor—intense and always upbeat.

STRADIVARIUS VIOLIN: Priceless, exquisite, soul-piercing—with the touch of the master.

FLUTTERING FLUTE: Tender, lighthearted, wide-ranging and clear as crystal.

SCOTTISH BAGPIPES: Forthright, distinctive and unmistakable.

SQUARE DANCE FIDDLE: Folksy, down-to-earth, toe-tapping—sprightly and full of energy.

ENCHANTING OBOE: Haunting, charming, disarming—even the cobra is harmless with this sound.

MELLOW CELLO: Deep, sonorous, compassionate—adding body and depth to the orchestra.

PIPE ORGAN: Grand, magnificent, rich—versatile and commanding.

HERALDING TRUMPET: Stirring, lively, invigorating—signaling attention and attack.

CLASSICAL GUITAR: Contemplative, profound, thoughtful *and* thought-provoking.

ONE-MAN BAND: Able to do many things well, all at once.

COMB AND TISSUE PAPER: Makeshift, original, uncomplicated—homespun and creative.

SWINGING TROMBONE: Warm, rich—great in solo or background support.

Broadway Show

Imagine for a moment that your group has been chosen to produce a Broadway show, and you have to choose people from your group for all of the jobs for this production. Have someone read out loud the job description for the first job below—PRODUCER. Then, let everyone in your group call out the name of the person in your group who would best fit this job. (You don't have to agree.) Then read the job description for the next job and let everyone nominate another person, etc. You only have 10 minutes for this assignment, so move fast.

PRODUCER: Typical Hollywood business tycoon; extravagant, big-budget, big-production magnate in the Steven Spielberg style.

DIRECTOR: Creative, imaginative brains who coordinates the production and draws the best out of others.

HEROINE: Beautiful, captivating, everybody's heart throb; defenseless when men are around, but nobody's fool.

HERO: Tough, macho, champion of the underdog, knight in shining armor; defender of truth.

COMEDIAN: Childlike, happy-go-lucky, outrageously funny, keeps everyone laughing.

CHARACTER PERSON: Rugged individualist, outrageously different, colorful, adds spice to any surrounding.

FALL GUY: Easy-going, nonchalant character who wins the hearts of everyone by being the "foil" of the heavy characters.

TECHNICAL DIRECTOR: The genius for "sound and lights"; creates the perfect atmosphere.

COMPOSER OF LYRICS: Communicates in music what everybody understands; heavy into feelings, moods, outbursts of energy.

PUBLICITY AGENT: Advertising and public relations expert; knows all the angles, good at one-liners, a flair for "hot" news.

VILLAIN: The "bad guy" who really is the heavy for the plot, forces others to think, challenges traditional values; out to destroy anything artificial or hypocritical.

AUTHOR: Shy, aloof; very much in touch with feelings, sensitive to people, puts into words what others only feel.

STAGEHAND: Supportive, behind-the-scenes person who makes things run smoothly; patient and tolerant.

Wild Predictions

Try to match the people in your group to the crazy forecasts below. (Don't take it too seriously; it's meant to be fun!) Read out loud the first item and ask everyone to call out the name of the person who is most likely to accomplish this feat. Then, read the next item and ask everyone to make a new prediction, etc.

THE PERSON IN OUR GROUP MOST LIKELY TO ...

Make a million selling Beanie Babies over the Internet

Become famous for designing new attire for sumo wrestlers

Replace Vanna White on *Wheel of Fortune*

Appear on *The Tonight Show* to exhibit an acrobatic talent

Move to a desert island

Discover a new use for underarm deodorant

Succeed David Letterman as host of *The Late Show*

Substitute for John Madden as Fox's football color analyst

Appear on the cover of *Muscle & Fitness Magazine*

Become the newest member of the Spice Girls

Work as a bodyguard for Rush Limbaugh at Feminist convention

Write a best-selling novel based on their love life

Be a dance instructor on a cruise ship for wealthy, well-endowed widows

Win the blue ribbon at the state fair for best Rocky Mountain oyster recipe

Land a job as head librarian for Amazon.com

Be the first woman to win the Indianapolis 500

Open the Clouseau Private Detective Agency

Career Placements

Read the list of career choices aloud and quickly choose someone in your group for each job—based upon their unique gifts and talents. Have fun!

SPACE ENVIRONMENTAL ENGINEER: in charge of designing the bathrooms on space shuttles

SCHOOL BUS DRIVER: for junior high kids in New York City (earplugs supplied)

WRITER: of an "advice to the lovelorn" column in Hollywood

SUPERVISOR: of a complaint department for a large automobile dealership and service department

ANIMAL PSYCHIATRIST: for French poodles in a fashionable suburb of Paris

RESEARCH SCIENTIST: studying the fertilization patterns of the dodo bird—now extinct

SAFARI GUIDE: in the heart of Africa—for wealthy widows and eccentric bachelors

LITTLE LEAGUE BASEBALL COACH: in Mudville, Illinois—last year's record was 0 and 12

MANAGER: of your local McDonald's during the holiday rush with 210 teenage employees

LIBRARIAN: for the Walt Disney Hall of Fame memorabilia

CHOREOGRAPHER: for the Dallas Cowboys cheerleaders

NURSE'S AIDE: at a home for retired Sumo wrestlers

SECURITY GUARD: crowd control officer at a rock concert

ORGANIZER: of paperwork for Congress

PUBLIC RELATIONS MANAGER: for Dennis Rodman

BODYGUARD: for Rush Limbaugh on a speaking tour of feminist groups

TOY ASSEMBLY PERSON: for a toy store over the holidays

You and Me, Partner

Think of the people in your group as you read over the list of activities below. If you had to choose someone from your group to be your partner, who would you choose to do these activities with? Jot down each person's name beside the activity. You can use each person's name only once and you have to use everyone's name once—so think it through before you jot down their names. Then, let one person listen to what others chose for them. Then, move to the next person, etc., around your group.

WHO WOULD YOU CHOOSE FOR THE FOLLOWING?

_____ ENDURANCE DANCE CONTEST partner

_____ BOBSLED RACE partner for the Olympics

_____ TRAPEZE ACT partner

_____ MY UNDERSTUDY for my debut in a Broadway musical

_____ BEST MAN or MAID OF HONOR at my wedding

_____ SECRET UNDERCOVER AGENT copartner

_____ BODYGUARD for me when I strike it rich

_____ MOUNTAIN CLIMBING partner in climbing Mt. Everest

_____ ASTRONAUT to fly the space shuttle while I walk in space

_____ SAND CASTLE TOURNAMENT building partner

_____ PIT CREW foreman for entry in Indianapolis 500

_____ AUTHOR for my biography

_____ SURGEON to operate on me for a life-threatening cancer

_____ NEW BUSINESS START-UP partner

_____ TAG-TEAM partner for a professional wrestling match

_____ HEAVY-DUTY PRAYER partner

My Gourmet Group

Here's a chance to pass out some much deserved praise for the people who have made your group something special. Ask one person to sit in silence while the others explain the delicacy they would choose to describe the contribution this person has made to your group. Repeat the process for each member of the group.

CAVIAR: That special touch of class and aristocratic taste that has made the rest of us feel like royalty.

PRIME RIB: Stable, brawny, macho, the generous mainstay of any menu; juicy, mouth-watering "perfect cut" for good nourishment.

IMPORTED CHEESE: Distinctive, tangy, mellow with age; adds depth to any meal.

VINEGAR AND OIL: Tart, witty, dry; a rare combination of healing ointment and pungent spice to add "bite" to the salad.

ARTICHOKE HEARTS: Tender and disarmingly vulnerable; whets the appetite for heartfelt sharing.

FRENCH PASTRY: Tempting, irresistible "creme de la creme" dessert; the connoisseur's delight for topping off a meal.

PHEASANT UNDER GLASS: Wild, totally unique, a rare dish for people who appreciate original fare.

CARAFE OF WINE: Sparkling, effervescent, exuberant and joyful; outrageously free and liberating to the rest of us.

ESCARGOT AND OYSTERS: Priceless treasures of the sea once out of their shells; succulent, delicate and irreplaceable.

FRESH FRUIT: Vine-ripened, energy-filled, invigorating; the perfect treat after a heavy meal.

ITALIAN ICE CREAMS: Colorful, flavorful, delightfully childlike; the unexpected surprise in our group.

Thank You

How would you describe your experience with this group? Choose one of the animals below that best describes how your experience in this group affected your life. Then share your responses with the group.

WILD EAGLE: You have helped to heal my wings, and taught me how to soar again.

TOWERING GIRAFFE: You have helped me to hold my head up and stick my neck out, and reach over the fences I have built.

PLAYFUL PORPOISE: You have helped me to find a new freedom and a whole new world to play in.

COLORFUL PEACOCK: You have told me that I'm beautiful; I've started to believe it, and it's changing my life.

SAFARI ELEPHANT: I have enjoyed this new adventure, and I'm not going to forget it, or this group; I can hardly wait for the next safari.

LOVABLE HIPPOPOTAMUS: You have let me surface and bask in the warm sunshine of God's love.

LANKY LEOPARD: You have helped me to look closely at myself and see some spots, and you still accept me the way I am.

DANCING BEAR: You have taught me to dance in the midst of pain, and you have helped me to reach out and hug again.

ALL-WEATHER DUCK: You have helped me to celebrate life—even in stormy weather—and to sing in the rain.

Academy Awards

You have had a chance to observe the gifts and talents of the members of your group. Now you will have a chance to pass out some much deserved praise for the contribution that each member of the group has made to your life. Read out loud the first award. Then let everyone nominate the person they feel is the most deserving for that award. Then read the next award, etc., through the list. Have fun!

SPARK PLUG AWARD: for the person who ignited the group

DEAR ABBY AWARD: for the person who cared enough to listen

ROYAL GIRDLE AWARD: for the person who supported us

WINNIE THE POOH AWARD: for the warm, caring person when someone needed a hug

ROCK OF GIBRALTER AWARD: for the person who was strong in the tough times of our group

OPRAH AWARD: for the person who asked the fun questions that got us to talk

TED KOPPEL AWARD: for the person who asked the heavy questions that made us think

KING ARTHUR'S AWARD: for the knight in shining armor

PINK PANTHER AWARD: for the detective who made us deal with Scripture

NOBEL PEACE PRIZE: for the person who harmonized our differences of opinion without diminishing anyone

BIG MAC AWARD: for the person who showed the biggest hunger for spiritual things

SERENDIPITY CROWN: for the person who grew the most spiritually during the course—in your estimation

You Remind Me of Jesus

Every Christian reflects the character of Jesus in some way. As your group has gotten to know each other, you can begin to see how each person demonstrates Christ in their very own personality. Go around the circle and have each person listen while others take turns telling that person what they notice in him or her that reminds them of Jesus. You may also want to tell them why you selected what you did.

YOU REMIND ME OF ...

JESUS THE HEALER: You seem to be able to touch someone's life with your compassion and help make them whole.

JESUS THE SERVANT: There's nothing that you wouldn't do for someone.

JESUS THE PREACHER: You share your faith in a way that challenges and inspires people.

JESUS THE LEADER: As Jesus had a plan for the disciples, you are able to lead others in a way that honors God.

JESUS THE REBEL: By doing the unexpected, you remind me of Jesus' way of revealing God in unique, surprising ways.

JESUS THE RECONCILER: Like Jesus, you have the ability to be a peacemaker between others.

JESUS THE TEACHER: You have a gift for bringing light and understanding to God's Word.

JESUS THE CRITIC: You have the courage to say what needs to be said, even if it isn't always popular.

JESUS THE SACRIFICE: Like Jesus, you seem willing to sacrifice anything to glorify God.

Reflections

Take some time to evaluate the life of your group by using the statements below. Read the first sentence out loud and ask everyone to explain where they would put a dot between the two extremes. When you are finished, go back and give your group an overall grade in the category of Group Building, Bible Study and Mission.

GROUP BUILDING

On celebrating life and having fun together, we were more like a ...
wet blanket _____ hot tub

On becoming a caring community, we were more like a ...
prickly porcupine _____ cuddly teddy bear

BIBLE STUDY

On sharing our spiritual stories, we were more like a ...
shallow pond _____ spring-fed lake

On digging into Scripture, we were more like a ...
slow-moving snail _____ voracious anteater

MISSION

On inviting new people into our group, we were more like a ...
barbed-wire fence _____ wide-open door

On stretching our vision for mission, we were more like an ...
ostrich _____ eagle

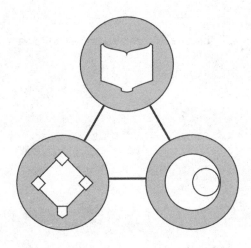

Human Bingo / Party Mixer

After the leader says "Go!" circulate the room, asking people the things described in the boxes. If someone answers "Yes" to a question, have them sign their initials in that box. Continue until someone completes the entire card—or one row if you don't have that much time. You can only use someone's name twice, and you cannot use your own name on your card.

can juggle	TP'd a house	never used an outhouse	sings in the shower	rec'd 6+ traffic tickets	paddled in school	watches Sesame Street
sleeps in church regularly	never changed a diaper	split pants in public	milked a cow	born out of the country	has been to Hawaii	can do the splits
watches soap operas	can touch tongue to nose	rode a motor-cycle	never ridden a horse	moved twice last year	sleeps on a waterbed	has hole in sock
walked in wrong restroom	loves classical music	skipped school	**FREE**	broke a leg	has a hot tub	loves eating sushi
is an only child	loves raw oysters	has a 3-inch + scar	doesn't wear PJ's	smoked a cigar	can dance the Charleston	weighs under 110 lbs.
likes writing poetry	still has tonsils	loves crossword puzzles	likes bubble baths	wearing Fruit of the Loom	doesn't use mouth-wash	often watches cartoons
kissed on first date	can wiggle ears	can play the guitar	plays chess regularly	reads the comics first	can touch palms to floor	sleeps with stuffed animal

Group Covenant

Any group can benefit from creating a group covenant. Reserve some time during one of the first meetings to discuss answers to the following questions. When everyone in the group has the same expectations for the group, everything runs more smoothly.

1. The purpose of our group is:

2. The goals of our group are:

3. We will meet for _____ weeks, after which we will decide if we wish to continue as a group. If we do decide to continue, we will reconsider this covenant.

4. We will meet _____ (weekly, every other week, monthly).

5. Our meetings will be from _____ o'clock to _____ o'clock, and we will strive to start and end on time.

6. We will meet at _____ or rotate from house to house.

7. We will take care of the following details: ❒ child care   ❒ refreshments

8. We agree to the following rules for our group:

   ❒ PRIORITY: While we are in this group, group meetings have priority.

   ❒ PARTICIPATION: Everyone is given the right to their own opinion and all questions are respected.

   ❒ CONFIDENTIALITY: Anything said in the meeting is not to be repeated outside the meeting.

   ❒ EMPTY CHAIR: The group stays open to new people and invites prospective members to visit the group.

   ❒ SUPPORT: Permission is given to call each other in times of need.

   ❒ ADVICE GIVING: Unsolicited advice is not allowed.

   ❒ MISSION: We will do all that is in our power to start a new group.

died a man, and that 'the Christ,' by which they meant a divine emanation, was within Him only during His public ministry, descending upon Him before the cross. They thus denied that Jesus was or is the Christ or the Son. They made Him a mere man invested for a brief period with divine powers or even adopted into the Godhead, but they denied that the man Jesus and the Eternal Son were and are the same Person, possessing two perfect natures, human and divine. In a word they denied the Incarnation" (Stott).

2:23 The Father and the Son are inseparable. To deny the Son is to deny the Father (despite what might be claimed). Likewise, to confess the Son is to confess the Father (see John 10:30). This is the awful effect of the secessionists' heresy: to deny Jesus makes fellowship with God impossible.

denies / acknowledges. These are the only two options when it comes to Jesus. The idea here is of public confession and public denial (see Matt. 10:32–33; John 12:42; Rom. 10:9–10).

2:24–27 "Here, then, are the two main safeguards against error—the apostolic Word and the anointing Spirit. Both are received at conversion. 'You have heard' the Word (v. 24) he says, and 'you received' (v. 27) the Spirit, although, indeed, he implies, the Word has come to you from us (1:2,3,5), while you have received the Spirit direct *of*, that is from, *him*, 'the Holy One' (vv. 20,27). The Word is an objective safeguard, while the anointing of the Spirit is a subjective experience; but both the apostolic teaching and the Heavenly Teacher are necessary for continuance in the truth. And both are to be personally and inwardly grasped" (Stott).

2:24 *See that.* John now issues a command. In the face of the lies of the antichrists they are to remain faithful to the Word of God.

what you have heard from the beginning. As an antidote to heresy, John urges his readers to let the original message which they heard right from the start of their Christian lives control their perspective. By urging them to remain faithful to the original apostolic word preached to them, he is ruling out private revelation that would deny or contradict this message—revelation such as the secessionists' new doctrines.

> *By God's grace, Christians remain faithful to the Word of God. Human response and divine activity are both part of the Christian life.*

remains. John's point is that when they remain in the truth they will remain in fellowship with God. To remain "expresses a continuing relationship. It is not enough merely to have heard and assented to the message in time past. The message must continue to be present and active in the lives of those who have heard it. They must continually call it to mind and let it affect their lives" (Marshall).

2:25 *eternal life.* What has been promised the Christian is the sharing of the very life of God—both now in the present (beginning at conversion) and on into the future after death (John 3:36; 6:40,47; 17:3).

2:26 *lead you astray.* John now reveals more about the secessionists. They were not simply content to leave the church and form their own fellowship based on their private doctrines. Instead, they actively sought to make converts from among the Christian community.

2:27 The ultimate safeguard against heresy is the Word of God which has been conveyed to their hearts by the Spirit with whom they have been anointed (Marshall).

remains in you. By God's grace, Christians remain faithful to the Word of God. Human response and divine activity are both part of the Christian life.

teach. John is not saying that after anointing by the Holy Spirit Christians need no more instruction. John, in fact, is instructing them via this letter! There are no "new" truths they need to learn besides what the apostles taught, and they certainly don't need any instruction by the false teachers.

all things. This is not "everything that can be known," but rather "all that you need to know."

6 Children of God—1 John 2:28–3:10

THREE-PART AGENDA

ICE-BREAKER
15 Minutes

BIBLE STUDY
30 Minutes

CARING TIME
15–45 Minutes

> *LEADER: Check page M7 in the center section for a good ice-breaker, particularly if you have a new person at this meeting. In the Caring Time, is everyone sharing and are prayer requests being followed up?*

TO BEGIN THE BIBLE STUDY TIME
(Choose 1 or 2)

1. Whose coming over would motivate you to get busy and clean house: Your boss? Your in-laws? This group? Other?

2. In your family, who is it said that you "take after" and why?

3. How did your parents or grandparents "spoil" you as you were growing up?

READ SCRIPTURE & DISCUSS
(If you don't have time for all the questions in this section, conclude the Bible Study [30 min.] by answering question #7.)

1. When you think of a group of people being led astray, what do you think of?

2. How would you feel if Christ returned right now: Excited? Relieved? Embarrassed? Afraid? Other?

3. What does it mean to be a child of God? What "hope" do the children of God have?

4. What do verses 1–3 tell us about God? How have you experienced God's lavish love?

Children of God

²⁸*And now, dear children, continue in him, so that when he appears we may be confident and unashamed before him at his coming.*

²⁹*If you know that he is righteous, you know that everyone who does what is right has been born of him.*

3 *How great is the love the Father has lavished on us, that we should be called children of God! And that is what we are! The reason the world does not know us is that it did not know him. ²Dear friends, now we are children of God, and what we will be has not yet been made known. But we know that when he appears,*ᵃ *we shall be like him, for we shall see him as he is. ³Everyone who has this hope in him purifies himself, just as he is pure.*

⁴*Everyone who sins breaks the law; in fact, sin is lawlessness. ⁵But you know that he appeared so that he might take away our sins. And in him is no sin. ⁶No one who lives in him keeps on sinning. No one who continues to sin has either seen him or known him.*

⁷*Dear children, do not let anyone lead you astray. He who does what is right is righteous, just as he is righteous. ⁸He who does what is sinful is of the devil, because the devil has been sinning from the beginning. The reason the Son of God appeared was to destroy the devil's work. ⁹No one who is born of God will continue to sin, because God's seed remains in him; he cannot go on sinning, because he has been born of God. ¹⁰This is how we know who the children of God are and who the children of the devil are: Anyone who does not do what is right is not a child of God; nor is anyone who does not love his brother.*

ᵃ2 Or *when it is made known*

5. What does John mean in verses 6 and 10 when he says that a Christian does not sin (see note on v. 6)?

6. What characteristics distinguish "the children of God" from "the children of the devil" (v. 10)?

7. This past week, did you feel more like a child of God or a distant relative? How can you improve your relationship with God this week?

CARING TIME

(Choose 1 or 2 of these questions before closing in prayer. Be sure to pray for the empty chair.)

1. It's not too late to have someone new come to this group. Who can you invite for next week?

2. Congratulations! You are over halfway through this study. What do you look forward to when you come to this group?

3. How would you like the group to pray for you this week?

Summary. In 1 John 2:18–27, John articulated the third and final test that distinguishes a cult from a Christian church. In the following passages (found in 2:28 to 4:6), he will go back over these three tests a second time. In this passage (2:28–3:10), he reexamines the moral test by discussing obedience once again. In 1 John 3:11–24, he reexamines the social test by discussing once again what is involved in loving other people. In 1 John 4:1–6, he reexamines the doctrinal test by pointing out again the correct view of Jesus.

2:28–3:3 Previously, John urged his readers to resist the proselytizing of the dissenters and to remain in Christ. In these verses, he continues to urge his readers to remain in Christ, but now the reason he gives has to do with the second coming of Christ. If they remain in Christ, when they meet the Lord at the Second Coming, they will not be ashamed. Instead, they will be confident before the Lord (2:28). Furthermore, they know that they will see Christ as he is and be made like him (3:2). The Second Coming is thus a source of great hope for the Christian and an encouragement to holy living (3:3).

2:28 *continue.* The word translated here as "continue" is the same Greek word that was translated "remain" in 2:19,24,27. It can be translated in a variety of ways: "to abide," "to remain steadfast," "to dwell," "to rest," "to persist," "to persevere," or "to be intimately united to." However, the best rendering is "to remain" or "to abide in."

confident and unashamed. On the Day of Judgment (which will occur at the Second Coming), those who have rejected Christ will feel a sense of unworthiness and shame in the presence of his holiness (Isa. 6:5), because of their open disgrace at having rejected Christ. In contrast, Christians will be able boldly to approach the royal presence because they have lived their lives in union with Christ.

2:29 *everyone who does what is right.* One consequence of spiritual rebirth is right living. It is, in fact, a sign of rebirth as the child begins to display the characteristics of his or her Heavenly Father.

born of him. Christians are those who experience "spiritual rebirth." John thus defines the relationship between the believer and God by means of the

analogy of the relationship between a child and a father (see also Titus 3:5; 1 Peter 1:3,23). One consequence of spiritual rebirth is right living. It is, in fact, a sign of rebirth as the child begins to display the characteristics of his or her Heavenly Father.

3:1 The precise nature of what Christians will become when they meet Christ is not fully clear ("what we will be has not yet been made known"). Yet they can get an idea of what they will be like by looking at Jesus ("we shall be like him"). In some way, Christians will become like Jesus when the process of glorification—which began at rebirth—is completed at the Second Coming.

> *One consequence of spiritual rebirth is right living. It is, in fact, a sign of rebirth as the child begins to display the characteristics of his or her Heavenly Father.*

3:3 *this hope.* Namely, that one day Christ will appear again at which time they will see him as he really is and be changed so as to become like him.

pure. This is a common word in the Bible denoting the outward purity required of those persons or objects involved in temple worship. In the usage here it speaks of the moral purity (freedom from sinning) that is required of Christians. Such purification is necessary for those who are in union with Christ. The secessionists, in contrast, were not much concerned about sin (1:5–2:2).

3:4–10 Having stated that those who are Christians have the hope of the Second Coming as their motivation for purifying themselves, John next looks at the sin from which they must purify themselves. In these verses he addresses the negative: the children of God must not sin. In 3:11–24 he will address the positive: instead, the children of God are to love one another.

3:4 *lawlessness.* It is not completely clear what John means when he says that "sin is lawlessness." Some scholars feel that what he is saying is that "sin consists of breaking the law of God." Other scholars feel—because of how this word is used in 2 Thessalonians 2:3,7—that what John is saying is "sin is placing oneself on the side of the 'man of lawlessness' " (i.e., Satan)—and thus standing in rebellion against God. Sin in this second sense is "siding with God's ultimate enemy!" (Marshall).

3:5 John gives yet another reason for not sinning. The very purpose for Jesus to come in the first place was to take away sin. So it is obvious that Jesus stands over against sin. Furthermore, there was no sin in Jesus' life. The implication is that those who are in union with Christ will reflect this same abhorrence of sin.

in him is no sin. John asserts that Jesus was sinless. His testimony is all the more powerful since this is not his main point. John is not trying to prove anything. He is simply stating what he knows to be true. And John was in a position to know whether Jesus was actually without sin because he lived with Jesus for some three years. Those who live with us know us best. Yet John says—after having seen Jesus in a variety of situations over a three-year period—that Jesus is *without sin.*

3:6 John appears to be saying here (and in vv. 8–10) that a Christian *cannot sin.* Yet in other passages, he points out that Christians can and do sin (e.g., 1:8,10; 2:1; 5:16). Some scholars feel that what John has in mind here is willful and deliberate sin (as against involuntary error). Other scholars stress the tense of the verb that John uses: a Christian does not *keep* on sinning. In other words, Christians do not habitually sin. Still other scholars feel that what John does here is to point out the ideal. This is what would happen if a Christian abided constantly in Christ. In any case, "John is arguing the incongruity rather than the impossibility of sin in the Christian" (Stott).

> **The very purpose for Jesus to come in the first place was to take away sin. So it is obvious that Jesus stands over against sin. Furthermore, there was no sin in Jesus' life.**

3:7 *lead you astray.* The secessionists deny that there is any incompatibility between being a Christian and continuing in sin. In other words, they not only seek to lead Christians away from the truth (2:26), they also seem to lead them into an immoral lifestyle.

3:8–10 In these verses John restates what he has said in verses 4–7. This statement parallels his previous statement except that here the focus is on the origin of sin (it is of the devil) rather than on the nature of sin (it is breaking the Law).

3:8 *sinful.* In verse 4, sinfulness was described as lawbreaking. Here sin is linked with Satan who from the beginning has sinned.

of the devil. Just as Christians display their Father's nature by moral living, so too others demonstrate by their immoral lifestyles that Satan is really their father.

3:9 *God's seed.* John probably is referring either to the Word of God (see Luke 8:11; James 1:18; 1 Peter 1:23) or to the Holy Spirit (see John 3:6) or to both, by which the Christian is kept from sin. In any case, "seed" is a metaphor for the indwelling power of God which brings forth new life.

cannot go on sinning. In 1:8,10 and 2:1, John attacks those who deny that they are sinners in need of forgiveness (i.e., those who are blind to the fact of their sin). Yet here he seems to say that Christians cannot sin. Some scholars feel that in chapter one John was responding to one aspect of the pre-Gnostic heresy of the secessionists—i.e., their teaching that those who were spiritually enlightened were perfect. But here he is dealing with a second aspect of that heresy—i.e., the teaching that sin did not matter. To those holding the first view he declared the universality of sin (all are sinners). Here, in the face of the second error, he declares the incompatibility of sin with the Christian life.

3:10 John here spells out in clear, unequivocal terms the moral test, although he casts it in negative terms: a person "who does not do right is not a child of God." He also articulates the social test—in anticipation of the next section—again in negative terms: a person "who does not love his brother" is not a child of God.

7 Love One Another—1 John 3:11–24

THREE-PART AGENDA

ICE-BREAKER
15 Minutes

BIBLE STUDY
30 Minutes

CARING TIME
15–45 Minutes

LEADER: Have you started working with your group about your mission— for instance, by having them review pages M3 and M6 in the center section? If you have a new person at the meeting, remember to do an appropriate ice-breaker from the center section.

TO BEGIN THE BIBLE STUDY TIME
(Choose 1 or 2)

1. Who was your first "crush"? What did you do to express your feelings for this person?

2. When has someone done something nice for you or your family when you were in need?

3. What lesson or saying from a parent, grandparent or teacher has stuck with you over the years?

READ SCRIPTURE & DISCUSS
(If you don't have time for all the questions in this section, conclude the Bible Study [30 min.] by answering question #7.)

1. Is it easier for you to express love for others more in words or in deeds?

2. How does "the world" define love? What is John's definition of love (vv. 16–18)?

3. In what ways does the world show hostility toward the righteous?

Love One Another

¹¹This is the message you heard from the beginning: We should love one another. ¹²Do not be like Cain, who belonged to the evil one and murdered his brother. And why did he murder him? Because his own actions were evil and his brother's were righteous. ¹³Do not be surprised, my brothers, if the world hates you. ¹⁴We know that we have passed from death to life, because we love our brothers. Anyone who does not love remains in death. ¹⁵Anyone who hates his brother is a murderer, and you know that no murderer has eternal life in him.

¹⁶This is how we know what love is: Jesus Christ laid down his life for us. And we ought to lay down our lives for our brothers. ¹⁷If anyone has material possessions and sees his brother in need but has no pity on him, how can the love of God be in him? ¹⁸Dear children, let us not love with words or tongue but with actions and in truth. ¹⁹This then is how we know that we belong to the truth, and how we set our hearts at rest in his presence ²⁰whenever our hearts condemn us. For God is greater than our hearts, and he knows everything.

²¹Dear friends, if our hearts do not condemn us, we have confidence before God ²²and receive from him anything we ask, because we obey his commands and do what pleases him. ²³And this is his command: to believe in the name of his Son, Jesus Christ, and to love one another as he commanded us. ²⁴Those who obey his commands live in him, and he in them. And this is how we know that he lives in us: We know it by the Spirit he gave us.

4. What are the results when Christians truly love others? What is the best example of love in action that you know?

5. In what ways do "our hearts condemn us" (v. 20)? How does it make you feel when you remember that God "knows everything" about you?

6. How is answered prayer connected to obedience (vv. 21–22)? How have you seen this to be true in your life?

7. What is a practical way this group can show God's love to another person in the coming week?

CARING TIME
(Choose 1 or 2 of these questions before closing in prayer. Be sure to pray for the empty chair.)

1. What is your dream for the future mission of this group?

2. Rate this past week on a scale of 1 (terrible) to 10 (great). What's the outlook for this week?

3. How can the group pray for you in the coming week?

Notes—1 John 3:11–24

Summary. The final verse of the previous session (3:10) links together the idea of righteousness and the idea of love. In that verse John says: "Anyone who does not do what is right is not a child of God; nor is anyone who does not love his brother." By this statement John moves from the first test of orthodoxy (the moral test) to the second test (the social test), which he expounds in verses 11–24. This passage has two parts to it. In part one (vv. 11–18), John states the second test: true Christians love one another. He demonstrates this first by the means of a negative example (Cain) and then by the means of a positive example (Jesus). Part two (vv. 19–24) is a parenthesis in the flow of his thought in which he comments on assurance and on obedience, both in the context of prayer.

3:11 *This is the message.* In 1:5 John used this same phrase to introduce the great truth that lies at the heart of the Christian message. God is light. Here he uses this phrase to introduce a second core insight: love is at the center of the Christian life. Those who seek to follow the God of light are called to a life of love.

you heard from the beginning. Once again (as in 2:7,24) John reminds his readers that it was the teaching of the apostles that initiated and nurtured their faith. In contrast, the secessionists are urging the Christian to accept "new and advanced" doctrine.

love one another. This is a restatement of the second test (see also 2:9–11). Genuine Christians are those whose aim it is to live a life of love for others.

3:12–15 John begins his exposition of love with a negative illustration: Cain's murder of his brother Abel.

> The human conscience is not infallible, but God is. The implication is that God—who knows a person's innermost secrets—will be more merciful than the heart of that person which sees in part and understands in part.

3:12 *belonged to the evil one.* Here John gives a specific example of what he meant in 3:8 when he said: "He who does what is sinful is of the devil." The killing of one's brother is the kind of evil that Satan inspires.

And why did he murder him? John answers this question in the next sentence: "Because his own actions were evil and his brother's were righteous." Cain knew that in contrast to his brother's gift, his offering to God did not arise out of the desire to do right. Therefore, because of his anger, Cain slew his brother.

3:13 Cain is an example of how evil hates righteousness. John warns the believers that wicked people will hate them too when they do good. The conclusion that John draws from this story is that Christians must expect hostility from the world (see 3:1 and John 15:18–25; 17:14; 1 Peter 4:12–19).

3:14 *death.* Here "death" refers to the kingdom of death—i.e., to the realm of Satan. In contrast, God's kingdom is characterized by life everlasting.

from death to life. The implication is that all people start out "dead." Satan is their father. They live in his realm. But by means of the rebirth process (which John mentioned in 2:29–3:2), it is possible to pass into the kingdom of life and become a child of God.

We know ... because we love. Love is evidence that one possesses eternal life.

3:15 *Anyone who hates his brother is a murderer.* Jesus makes this same link between hatred and murder (see Matt. 5:21–22). However, Jesus stopped short of saying what John does, namely that hatred is tantamount to murder.

3:16–17 John next offers a positive example of love: Jesus' sacrificial love for the human race. Both the example of Cain and the example of Jesus involve death. But Cain's act sprang from hatred and *took* the life of another while Jesus' act sprang from love and he *gave* his own life for others.

3:16 *This is how we know what love is.* John defines "love" not by means of an intellectual proposition, but by a practical example. Love is what Jesus demonstrated when he gave his life for others.

3:17 While only a few Christians will be called upon to make the supreme sacrifice of their lives for the sake of others, *all* Christians can and must constantly share their possessions in order to relieve the material suffering that abounds in this world.

brother. In verse 16 John used the plural "brothers." But here he becomes quite specific and asks his readers to consider the needs of a particular individual ("brother" is singular). "Loving everyone in general may be an excuse for loving nobody in particular" (Lewis).

pity. Such self-giving love is not without emotion, even though it is not primarily a feeling. John calls for genuine concern and caring in the face of the plight of others.

3:18 But this "love" must be more than the mere verbal affirmation that, "Yes, I am committed to the idea of love." Genuine love shows itself in concrete deeds and in truth.

3:19–24 This section is a parenthesis in John's thought by which he both concludes the previous section and provides a bridge to the new section. It is not easy, however, to follow John's thought-flow here as he links together the human and the divine aspects of assurance. The important thing to notice is that he is talking about prayer.

3:19–20 John seems to be saying that Christians can be at peace with themselves even when their consciences trouble them. Such troubled consciences may be the result of introspection that has pointed out how feeble their attempts are to love others and how prone to sin they seem to be. But, as John points out, the basis of their confidence is the fact that it is God who will judge them and not their own hearts. They can trust themselves to his all-knowing justice because they have sought and found his forgiveness (see 1 Cor. 4:3–5).

3:19 truth. By this word John links this new section to the previous section. People can only "belong to the truth" (v. 19)—i.e., be a part of God's kingdom, when they act "in truth" (v. 18)—i.e., when they love genuinely.

3:20 he knows everything. The human conscience is not infallible, but God is. The implication is that God—who knows a person's innermost secrets—will be more merciful than the heart of that person which sees in part and understands in part.

> *Confidence is necessary in order to come before God. Without confidence a person does not feel free to enter into prayer.*

3:21 confidence. Confidence is necessary in order to come before God. Without confidence a person does not feel free to enter into prayer.

3:22 Once again, John states a truth in a stark, unqualified way: if we ask, we will receive. Later, however, he will add the stipulation that people must ask "according to [God's] will" (5:14).

obey. Obedience is not the cause of answered prayer; it is the condition that motivates Christians to pray. Obedience is the evidence that they are moving in accordance with God's will, that they are in union with him, and that they will want to pray.

3:23–24 In these verses, John brings together the three issues which underlie the three tests by which believers can know they are truly children of God. He shows the interconnection between obedience (the moral test), love (the social test), and belief (the doctrinal test) and how these relate to the question of union with God.

3:24 Those who obey his commands live in him. Obedience and union are connected. God's command is to believe and love. Obedience to this command brings union with Christ. Looked at from the other way around, union brings the desire and the ability to obey. In other words, the outward, objective side of the Christian life (which is active love for others in obedience to the command of God) is connected to the inner, subjective experience of being in union with God.

8 Test the Spirits—1 John 4:1–6

THREE-PART AGENDA

ICE-BREAKER
15 Minutes

BIBLE STUDY
30 Minutes

CARING TIME
15–45 Minutes

> **LEADER: To help you identify an Apprentice / Leader for a new small group (or if you have a new person at this meeting), see the listing of ice-breakers on page M7 of the center section.**

TO BEGIN THE BIBLE STUDY TIME
(Choose 1 or 2)

1. Do you prefer multiple-choice or essay tests? What is the last big test you had to take?

2. How do you stay informed on current events? How confident are you of the accuracy of the sources you use?

3. What's the strangest religious group or cult you've ever heard of?

READ SCRIPTURE & DISCUSS
(If you don't have time for all the questions in this section, conclude the Bible Study [30 min.] by answering question #7.)

1. If you were to ask the average person who they thought Jesus was, what answers might you be likely to get?

2. Name some examples of "false prophets" down through the ages.

3. In this passage, what is said about spirits and how we can distinguish between true and false spirits? In what circumstance might it be necessary for you to distinguish between spirits?

Test the Spirits

4 *Dear friends, do not believe every spirit, but test the spirits to see whether they are from God, because many false prophets have gone out into the world. ²This is how you can recognize the Spirit of God: Every spirit that acknowledges that Jesus Christ has come in the flesh is from God, ³but every spirit that does not acknowledge Jesus is not from God. This is the spirit of the antichrist, which you have heard is coming and even now is already in the world.*

⁴You, dear children, are from God and have overcome them, because the one who is in you is greater than the one who is in the world. ⁵They are from the world and therefore speak from the viewpoint of the world, and the world listens to them. ⁶We are from God, and whoever knows God listens to us; but whoever is not from God does not listen to us. This is how we recognize the Spirit^a of truth and the spirit of falsehood.

^a6 Or *spirit*

4. What does John mean by "the spirit of the antichrist ... is already in the world" (v. 3)?

5. How are children of God able to overcome the spirits of the world?

6. When has the "spirit of falsehood" (v. 6) affected your life?

7. What is the lesson in this passage for you?

CARING TIME
(Choose 1 or 2 of these questions before closing in prayer.)

1. If this group is helping hold you accountable for something, how are you doing in that area? If not, what is something for which you would like this group to hold you accountable?

2. Have you started to work on your group mission—to choose an Apprentice / Leader from this group to start a new group in the future? (See Mission / Multiplication on page M3).

3. In what specific way can the group pray for you this week?

Summary. In the final verse of the previous session, John describes how Christians can know that God lives in them. They know this because the Holy Spirit bears inner witness to this fact (3:24). But the problem is that the secessionists make this same claim! They say that God's Spirit speaks to them, too. In fact, such private revelations are the source of their new doctrine. So, how can one distinguish between spirits? What is the difference between God's Spirit and false spirits? Is there an objective basis on which to accept or reject subjective claims? The answer relates to doctrine. That spirit which acknowledges that Jesus (the Messiah) came in the flesh is a spirit from God. Likewise, the opposite is true. Those spirits that do not acknowledge Jesus in this way are not from God (see also 2:20–23).

Thus, in this passage, John expands on the doctrinal test—the third way by which to distinguish between true and false Christianity. There are two parts to this test. The first question is: to what spirit does one listen? Unless that spirit acknowledges Jesus as the Messiah come in the flesh, it is not of God (v. 2). The second question is: are you in submission to apostolic doctrine? Unless individuals acknowledge and recognize the truth of the Gospel (as taught from the beginning by apostles such as John), they are not following "the Spirit of truth" (v. 6).

4:1 *do not believe every spirit.* Having just claimed that Christians know God lives in them because the Holy Spirit bears witness to this fact, John hastens on to qualify what he means. Not everything a spirit says is automatically of God. In fact, it is dangerous to accept uncritically everything that is said "in the name of God." Not everyone claiming inner revelation is hearing God's voice!

test. The test that John suggests by which to distinguish between spirits is doctrinal in nature. It has to do with who Jesus is. False spirits will not acknowledge that Jesus of Nazareth (a fully human man) is the incarnate Christ (the divine Son of God). Notice that the focus of this test is upon the *spirit* who is the source of the prophecy—not upon what is said. In other words, true prophecy is not distinguished from false prophecy by the content of the prophecy itself. The question is: is the source of this prophecy divine or diabolical? (See also 1 Cor. 12:1–3; 14:29; 1 Thessalonians 5:19–22.)

spirits. The issue is not whether supernatural spirits exist and actually inspire prophecy. This was assumed to be the case by almost everyone in the first century (see, for example, Mark 1:21–28, 32–34). The question Christians wrestled with was how to know what kind of spirit was speaking in any given situation. Are the secessionists telling the truth? Have they heard a fresh word from God? Did the Holy Spirit inspire this new doctrine? John provides them with a means whereby they can tell the difference between God's Spirit and false spirits.

> *Not everything a spirit says is automatically of God. In fact, it is dangerous to accept uncritically everything that is said "in the name of God." Not everyone claiming inner revelation is hearing God's voice!*

from God. John uses this phrase in five of the six verses in this unit. By it, in verses 1–3, he seeks to indicate that certain spirits have their origin in God (as opposed to others that emanate from "the antichrist") and in verses 4 and 6 he points out that certain people are from God (as opposed to others who are "from the world").

prophets. Prophets are those men and women who claim to speak on God's behalf. They allow the Holy Spirit—or another spirit—to speak through them. John does not deny the reality or the value of prophecy. He simply warns against false prophets, much as Jesus did (see Matt. 7:15; Mark 13:22–23).

4:2 To deny that Jesus, the Messiah, was truly human is incompatible with divine inspiration. Prophets who will not affirm this confession of faith are not of God.

acknowledges. What John has in mind is not mere recognition of who Jesus is—since even the demons know him (Mark 1:24). Rather, what is called for is an open, positive, public declaration of faith in Jesus.

Jesus Christ has come in the flesh. This is the second of three places in this epistle in which John touches upon how the secessionists view the person of Jesus. In 2:22–23, John says that they deny that Jesus is the Christ (i.e., that he is the Messiah). (See note on 2:22 in Session 5.) Here he asserts that they deny that Jesus, the Messiah, came in the flesh. In 5:6 (the third and final place at which he deals with the question of Jesus' nature), John gets to the heart of the matter. What the secessionists are really denying is that Jesus—as the Messiah—could have died.

4:3 In verse 2 John focused on the positive: Those spirits who acknowledge Jesus are from God. Here he focuses on the negative: Those who do not acknowledge Jesus are not from God.

antichrist. John returns to a theme he first dealt with in 2:18–27 (see the notes on 2:18 in Session 5). In that section John's concern was that believers not be led astray by those who are filled with the spirit of the antichrist. Here his concern is with the claims by his opponents that their new teachings are inspired by God.

4:4–6 John turns from his focus on prophets (true and false) to a consideration of those who follow each type of prophet. In verse 4 he directs his word to "you" (the Christians in Ephesus); in verse 5 he talks about "them" and "they" (the secessionists); while in verse 6 he talks about "we" (the apostles, of whom John is a representative).

4:4 overcome. The Christians to whom John writes have successfully resisted overtures by false prophets (the secessionists) to get them to believe new doctrines. They have not been deceived.

the one who is in you. It is not by means of their own unaided strength that they are able to resist these false prophets. The source of their power is the Spirit of God who resides in them.

the one who is in the world. Satan is the power at work in the world.

4:5 The false prophets, having been inspired by Satan, are readily heard and accepted by those who are likewise influenced by Satan.

4:6 In contrast to the "world" (which stands in opposition to God, God's truth, and God's people), there is the church (which both believes God's truth and seeks to live it out).

We / us. Since John shifts from "you" in verse 4 to "we" in verse 6 it would appear that here he has in mind not just Christians in general but, specifically, teachers of apostolic doctrine like himself. This is the only unambiguous criterion for truth that John offers: "We are from God and whoever knows God listens to us." Those who follow John and other teachers of apostolic doctrine are following the "Spirit of truth." While it is true the Spirit affirms what is truth for those who know God, the fact is that the secessionists also claim to be led by the Spirit. So this criterion for knowing who is really following God is, by itself, ambiguous. However, the secessionists do not follow John and on this basis are quite clearly outside the bounds of apostolic Christianity.

Spirit of truth. Those who respond positively to the apostolic preaching are those who are led by "the Spirit of truth"—a reference probably to the Holy Spirit.

9 God's Love & Ours—1 John 4:7–21

THREE-PART AGENDA

ICE-BREAKER
15 Minutes

BIBLE STUDY
30 Minutes

CARING TIME
15–45 Minutes

 LEADER: *To help you identify people who might form the core of a new small group (or if a new person comes to this meeting), see the listing of ice-breakers on page M7 of the center section.*

TO BEGIN THE BIBLE STUDY TIME
(Choose 1 or 2)

1. As a child, how did you react when something frightened you in the middle of the night?

2. What token or memento of love have you kept that is especially meaningful to you?

3. How would you finish the sentence: "Love is like ..."?

READ SCRIPTURE & DISCUSS
(If you don't have time for all the questions in this section, conclude the Bible Study [30 min.] by answering question #7.)

1. What love story (real or fictional) has been an example to you of true love?

2. If you were to summarize this passage in one sentence, what would you say?

3. How has God demonstrated that he is love (v. 8)? How can a person know God and experience his love?

4. From verses 8–15, what do you learn about the relationship between the Father, Son and Holy Spirit?

God's Love and Ours

*⁷Dear friends, let us love one another, for love comes from God. Everyone who loves has been born of God and knows God. ⁸Whoever does not love does not know God, because God is love. ⁹This is how God showed his love among us: He sent his one and only Son*ᵃ *into the world that we might live through him. ¹⁰This is love: not that we loved God, but that he loved us and sent his Son as an atoning sacrifice for* ᵇ *our sins. ¹¹Dear friends, since God so loved us, we also ought to love one another. ¹²No one has ever seen God; but if we love one another, God lives in us and his love is made complete in us.*

¹³We know that we live in him and he in us, because he has given us of his Spirit. ¹⁴And we have seen and testify that the Father has sent his Son to be the Savior of the world. ¹⁵If anyone acknowledges that Jesus is the Son of God, God lives in him and he in God. ¹⁶And so we know and rely on the love God has for us.

God is love. Whoever lives in love lives in God, and God in him. ¹⁷In this way, love is made complete among us so that we will have confidence on the day of judgment, because in this world we are like him. ¹⁸There is no fear in love. But perfect love drives out fear, because fear has to do with punishment. The one who fears is not made perfect in love.

¹⁹We love because he first loved us. ²⁰If anyone says, "I love God," yet hates his brother, he is a liar. For anyone who does not love his brother, whom he has seen, cannot love God, whom he has not seen. ²¹And he has given us this command: Whoever loves God must also love his brother.

ᵃ9 Or *his only begotten Son*   ᵇ10 Or *as the one who would turn aside his wrath, taking away*

5. What fears keep people from loving God or others? In what way does "perfect love" (v. 18) drive out fear?

6. What is the connection between God's love for us and the love we are to have for others?

7. How can being mindful of God's love for you help you in the week ahead?

CARING TIME
(Choose 1 or 2 of these questions before closing in prayer.)

1. Who would you choose as the leader if this group "gave birth" to a new small group? Who else would you choose to be a part of the leadership core for a new group?

2. How are you doing at spending personal time in prayer and Bible Study?

3. What prayer needs or praises would you like to share?

Summary. In 3:23 John stated, "This is his command: to believe in the name of his Son, Jesus Christ, and to love one another as he commanded us." In the previous passage (4:1–6), John expanded on the first part of this command—believing in Jesus. In verses 7–21 he expands on the second part of the command—loving other people. John uses the word "love" some 43 times in his epistle; 27 of those times are in this passage.

> *Christians have the Holy Spirit because they acknowledge that Jesus is the Son of God and because they dwell in his unconditional love.*

4:7 For the third time John returns to the theme of love. In his first discussion he reminded his readers that love is a command and that to love is to live in the light (2:7–11). In his second discussion he pointed out that Jesus is the model of how to love others and that loving others is evidence that a person belongs to the truth (3:11–20). In this discussion he points out the basis on which he has said all this about love. It is because God himself is love!

love one another. John will use this phrase three times in the next five verses (see vv. 7,11,12). Each time, however, he uses it in a slightly different way. Here he urges his readers to love others because love originates in God.

Everyone who loves. Since "love comes from God," all acts of love are reflections of God's nature.

4:8 *Whoever does not love does not know God.* To claim to be a Christian without living a life of love "is like claiming to be intimate with a foreigner whose language we cannot speak, or to have been born of parents whom we do not in any way resemble" (Stott). Love is the language of God and the mark of his parentage.

God is love. This is the second great assertion that John makes in this epistle about the nature of God. (His first assertion is that God is light.) In the first cen-

tury both these statements about God would have been unexpected. At that time in history there was a deep suspicion that the gods were dark and mysterious and that they cared little about human beings.

4:9–10 John now underlines what he said previously, both in his Gospel (John 3:16) and in this epistle (1 John 3:16): true love expresses itself in self-sacrificial action undertaken for the benefit of another person without regard to personal cost.

4:10 Love is initiated by God. Love is his posture toward the human race, and this love is given substance by the incarnation of his Son. It is not the other way around. People do not reach out to God with warm feelings or acts of devotion and thereby trigger his love for them. God is the primal lover. It is his action that draws out their response. Love begins with God.

an atoning sacrifice for our sins. By this phrase John describes the saving work that Jesus did on behalf of the human race. The idea of atonement is tied up with the Old Testament concept of substitution and sacrifice. In the Old Testament, sin was dealt with when a person symbolically placed his sins on an animal that he had brought to the temple. This animal had to be perfect—without spot or blemish. It was then sacrificed in place of the sinful (imperfect) person. Such substitutionary sacrifices were a picture of the final sacrifice Jesus would one day make for all men and women.

4:11 *love one another.* This is the second time John uses this phrase. The basis for his exhortation this time is the demonstrated fact that "God so loved us." Jesus' sacrificial death on behalf of the human race assures people that God loves them, and thus releases in them the ability to love others. Because they are loved they can love.

4:12 *No one has ever seen God.* It is not possible for a human being to see God in a direct, unscreened way. Such an encounter is beyond human capability. John reiterates here (and elsewhere) the biblical teachings on this matter. (See John 1:18; 5:37; 6:46; as well as Exodus 33:19–23.) Perhaps John finds it necessary to say this because some of the secessionists claim to have seen God.

love one another. In the third use of this phrase, John states that although God cannot be seen directly, his life can be experienced by people as they love one another. Since God is love, they know him when they love.

4:13–16 In these verses John elaborates on the phrase in verse 12: "God lives in us."

4:14–16 Christians have the Holy Spirit (v. 13) because they acknowledge that Jesus is the Son of God (vv. 14–15) and because they dwell in his unconditional love (v. 16).

4:17–21 Having completed his comments on what the statement means that "God lives in us," John next elaborates on a second phrase from verse 12: "his love is made complete in us."

4:17 confidence. Just as believers will have confidence at the second coming of Christ (2:28) and as they have confidence when they approach God in prayer (3:19–22), so too they will also have confidence on the Day of Judgment.

we are like him. Once again—as he did in 3:6 and 9—John speaks about a future reality as if it were even now fully realized. In fact, as he has already stated (3:2), believers will not "be like him" until the Second Coming.

4:18 no fear in love. The reason for the confidence believers will have on the Day of Judgment is that they know God to be their father in whose love they have trusted. People cannot love and fear at the same moment; i.e., it is impossible to approach God with a heart filled both with servile fear and with an overflowing sense of his love for them and their love for him. The love casts out the fear.

fear has to do with punishment. This is the root of the fear: they think God is going to punish them. They forget that they are his forgiven children.

4:19 The love believers exhibit is a response to the prior love of God for them. Love begets love.

4:20 Love for God is not merely warm, inner feelings. Love is not love unless it finds concrete expression via active caring for others. Furthermore, since it is far easier to love a visible person than to love the invisible God, to claim success in the harder task (loving God) while failing in the easier task (loving others) is an absurd and hopeless contradiction.

a liar. Three times in this letter John has pointed out lies. It is a lie to claim to follow God and yet live in darkness by not keeping his commands (1:6; 2:4). It is a lie to claim God as Father while denying Jesus his Son (2:22–23). And here he says that it is a lie to claim to love God while hating others. These three lies parallel the three tests of a true Christian. The three lies are the reverse side of the moral, doctrinal and relational tests. The true Christian does not live in an immoral fashion, does not deny Jesus and does not hate others. Holiness, faith and love verify the claim to be a child of God.

4:21 If people truly love God they will keep his commands; and his command is to love others—as John reminds his readers one more time as he ends this lesson on love (see also 2:9–11; 3:10,23). To love God and to love others is a single inseparable ordinance.

> *Love is initiated by God. Love is his posture toward the human race, and this love is given substance by the incarnation of his Son. It is not the other way around. People do not reach out to God with warm feelings or acts of devotion and thereby trigger his love for them. God is the primal lover. It is his action that draws out their response. Love begins with God.*

10 Faith in Jesus—1 John 5:1–12

THREE-PART AGENDA

ICE-BREAKER
15 Minutes

BIBLE STUDY
30 Minutes

CARING TIME
15–45 Minutes

> *LEADER: Has your group discussed its plans on what to study after this course is finished? What about the mission project described on page M6 in the center section?*

TO BEGIN THE BIBLE STUDY TIME
(Choose 1 or 2)

1. At what age did you stop believing in Santa Claus and why?

2. As a teenager, what rule did your parents enforce that you found most burdensome: Curfew? Use of the car? What friends you could associate with? Other?

3. What question are you anxious to ask God someday?

READ SCRIPTURE & DISCUSS
(If you don't have time for all the questions in this section, conclude the Bible Study [30 min.] by answering question #7.)

1. What bad habit or difficult situation have you overcome? How did you do it?

2. Why are God's commands "not burdensome" (v. 3)? What is the difference between something being difficult and being a burden?

3. What are the three witnesses to Jesus Christ? In what way did Jesus come "by water and blood" (v. 6)?

4. What testimony does God give about his Son?

Faith in the Son of God

5 *Everyone who believes that Jesus is the Christ is born of God, and everyone who loves the father loves his child as well. ²This is how we know that we love the children of God: by loving God and carrying out his commands. ³This is love for God: to obey his commands. And his commands are not burdensome, ⁴for everyone born of God overcomes the world. This is the victory that has overcome the world, even our faith. ⁵Who is it that overcomes the world? Only he who believes that Jesus is the Son of God.*
⁶This is the one who came by water and blood—Jesus Christ. He did not come by water only, but by water and blood. And it is the Spirit who testifies, because the Spirit is the truth. ⁷For there are three that testify: ⁸the^a Spirit, the water and the blood; and the three are in agreement. ⁹We accept man's testimony, but God's testimony is greater because it is the testimony of God, which he has given about his Son. ¹⁰Anyone who believes in the Son of God has this testimony in his heart. Anyone who does not believe God has made him out to be a liar, because he has not believed the testimony God has given about his Son. ¹¹And this is the testimony: God has given us eternal life, and this life is in his Son. ¹²He who has the Son has life; he who does not have the Son of God does not have life.

a 7,8 Late manuscripts of the Vulgate *testify in heaven: the Father, the Word and the Holy Spirit, and these three are one.* 8 *And there are three that testify on earth: the* (not found in any Greek manuscript before the sixteenth century)

5. When did you come to believe "that Jesus is the Son of God" (v. 5)? What change has this made in your life?

6. From this passage, what would you say to a friend who has doubts they are really a Christian?

7. How can you use *your* testimony to help someone know the truth?

CARING TIME
(Answer all the questions that follow, then close in prayer.)

1. Next week will be your last session in this study. How would you like to celebrate: A dinner? A party? Other?

2. What is the next step for this group: Start a new group? Continue with another study?

3. What prayer requests do you have for this week?

(If the group plans to continue, see the back inside cover of this book for what's available from Serendipity.)

Notes—1 John 5:1–12

Summary. John has one last statement to make before he concludes his book. It has to do with Jesus. The crucial issue in this whole matter of orthodoxy versus apostasy hinges on one's view of Jesus. If faith is rightly directed at the historic Jesus, then (by implication) correct lifestyle and loving relationships will flow from that commitment. But if not— if the Jesus who is honored is more a product of fancy than fact—then quite a different worldview will flourish (as the secessionists demonstrate). So John ends where he began—with his testimony to Jesus.

In his final argument, John returns to the themes he struck in his prologue. The parallels between his first and last statements are strong. For example, in the prologue John spoke about testifying, "The life appeared; we have seen it and testify to it ..." (1:2). "Testimony" is also a key theme in this passage. In the prologue, John spoke about eternal life: "... we proclaim to you the eternal life" (1:2). (The word "life" appeared there three times.) Here also one finds the concept of eternal life. (The word "life" is used four times in 5:4–12.)

> *It is by means of faith in Jesus that Christians can win over the world which stands in opposition to them as they seek to follow the ways of God.*

5:1–4a Here John ties together the three tests of faith. "The real link between the three tests is seen to be the new birth. Faith, love and obedience are the natural outgrowth which follows a birth from above" (Stott).

5:1 *believes.* The tense of the verb (in Greek) indicates that belief is here seen as the result of new birth, not its cause. The belief on the part of Christians is clear proof that they have been born of God. However, elsewhere John points to faith as the condition of the new birth (John 1:12). The two emphases are complementary: faith enables the new birth to happen and faith is the sign that new birth has taken place.

5:3 *burdensome.* Obedience to the thousands of often picayune rules and regulations promulgated by the scribes and Pharisees was indeed a heavy burden. But obedience to God does not exasperate the Christian, since God's laws are of quite a different character (e.g., they are life-giving), and the faith of Christians provides the power for obedience.

5:4 *has overcome the world.* To the world, God's commands are a burden (v. 3); but not to Christians who by virtue of the new birth live in a new sphere. But what is this "victory that has overcome the world"? John might have in mind the past victory of Jesus via his death and resurrection (see John 16:33). In this case, Christians would participate in that victory by continuing to win over the world through the power of Jesus. Or John may have in view the conversion of each believer, which would be the moment he or she entered into the conquering power of Jesus. In either case, it is Jesus who has won the victory and Christians who continue to participate in it.

our faith. This is the source of the overcoming power of the Christian—confidence and trust that Jesus is the Son of God (see 5:5). It is by means of faith in Jesus that Christians can win over the world which stands in opposition to them as they seek to follow the ways of God.

5:6–9 How is it that a person comes to faith in Jesus? By means of reliable witnesses, John answers. In these verses he names three such witnesses that testify to who Jesus is and what he has done. These three witnesses are the water, the blood and the Holy Spirit.

5:6 *by water and blood.* By these two phrases, John probably is referring to Jesus' baptism and Jesus' death. These two events are crucial in understanding who Jesus really is. The secessionists felt that Jesus, the man, became the Christ at his baptism and that the Christ then departed prior to the death of Jesus. In contrast, the apostolic witness (as recorded in the New Testament) asserts that at his baptism, Jesus publicly identified himself with the sins of the people (even though he himself was without sin). And at his death, Jesus died to take away those sins. Water and blood also function as symbols of purification and redemption. This was their meaning in the rituals described in Leviticus.

Furthermore, they would also remind John's readers of the ordinances of baptism and communion. Some scholars feel that the "water and the blood" refer to the single event of the Crucifixion during which "water and blood" flowed from the side of Jesus.

Jesus Christ. So as to drive home his point, John uses this dual title which displays the inextricable unity of the divine and human in this one person. He is Jesus of Nazareth and he is the Messiah sent by God. It was Jesus Christ—and not just a human named Jesus—who experienced both baptism and death.

not ... by water only. The secessionists agree that the baptism of Jesus was all important. They felt it was then that the heavenly Christ infused the man Jesus. (In fact, it was the Holy Spirit who descended on Jesus at his baptism.) John is insistent that both the Baptism and the Crucifixion are crucial in understanding Jesus. If it was only a human named Jesus who died on the cross (as John's opponents thought), then universal forgiveness for sin would be impossible. But, in fact, it was Jesus, *the Messiah*, who died on the cross. Furthermore, it would be a lie that God sent his only Son to die for the world (as John states in his Gospel in 3:16), if it had been only a human named Jesus who was crucified.

it is the Spirit who testifies. John has already stated that there is an inner witness given by the Holy Spirit as to the truth of who Jesus is (see 3:24 and 4:13 as well as 1 Cor. 12:3). In verses 6–11, John will use the verb "to testify, or bear witness" four times and the noun "testimony or witness" six times.

the Spirit is the truth. The Holy Spirit is the third witness, and is qualified to be such because the Spirit is, in his essence, truth itself.

5:7 three that testify. There are two kinds of testimony: the objective historical witness of the water and the blood (Jesus identified himself with the sins of the people at his baptism and then died for these sins on the cross); and the subjective, experiential witness of the Spirit (Christians experience within themselves the reality of these events). These two types of witness complement one another. Believers know in their hearts the truthfulness and power of the historical facts of Jesus' life and death.

5:9 John now clarifies the authority behind these three witnesses. It is God himself. In addition, the object of the three-fold witness is made explicit. It is Jesus his Son.

> *It is one thing to BELIEVE Jesus. It is another to BELIEVE IN Jesus. To believe Jesus is to accept what he says as true. To believe in Jesus is to accept who he is. It is to trust him completely and to commit one's life to him.*

greater. In a law court, testimony is accepted when it is corroborated by two or three witnesses (see Deut. 19:15). How much more substantial is the three-fold testimony of God?

5:10–12 Here John points out the result of believing this triple testimony. The believer gains eternal life. The purpose of this testimony is to produce faith. To accept the testimony is synonymous with believing in Jesus.

5:10 believes in. It is one thing to *believe* Jesus. It is another to *believe in* Jesus. To believe Jesus is to accept what he says as true. To believe in Jesus is to accept who he is. It is to trust him completely and to commit one's life to him.

a liar. To reject this triple testimony is to disbelieve God (who is himself the essence of truth). It is to attribute falsehood to God (see 1:10).

5:11 eternal life. In receiving the testimony and thus receiving the Son, one also receives eternal life. The Greek word which is here translated "eternal" means "that which belongs to the coming age." But since that age has already broken into the present age, eternal life can be enjoyed even now.

11 Concluding Remarks—1 John 5:13–21

THREE-PART AGENDA

ICE-BREAKER
15 Minutes

BIBLE STUDY
30 Minutes

CARING TIME
15–45 Minutes

 LEADER: Check page M7 of the center section for a good ice-breaker for this last session.

TO BEGIN THE BIBLE STUDY TIME
(Choose 1 or 2)

1. Growing up, who was your "idol"—someone you admired and wanted to be like?

2. If you saw someone littering, what would you likely do: Confront them? Tell someone else? Ignore it?

3. What would you like to thank God for today?

READ SCRIPTURE & DISCUSS
(If you don't have time for all the questions in this section, conclude the Bible Study [30 min.] by answering question #7.)

1. How has this group, or someone in the group, been a blessing to you over the course of this study?

2. From this passage, what things can a Christian "know" (vv. 13,15,18,19,20)? In what ways does this knowledge encourage you today?

3. What is the confidence we should have when we pray to God? On a scale of 1 (low) to 10 (high), how does your "confidence meter" read?

4. How are we to help fellow Christians who struggle with sin?

Concluding Remarks

¹³*I write these things to you who believe in the name of the Son of God so that you may know that you have eternal life. ¹⁴This is the confidence we have in approaching God: that if we ask anything according to his will, he hears us. ¹⁵And if we know that he hears us—whatever we ask—we know that we have what we asked of him.*

¹⁶If anyone sees his brother commit a sin that does not lead to death, he should pray and God will give him life. I refer to those whose sin does not lead to death. There is a sin that leads to death. I am not saying that he should pray about that. ¹⁷All wrongdoing is sin, and there is sin that does not lead to death.

¹⁸We know that anyone born of God does not continue to sin; the one who was born of God keeps him safe, and the evil one cannot harm him. ¹⁹We know that we are children of God, and that the whole world is under the control of the evil one. ²⁰We know also that the Son of God has come and has given us understanding, so that we may know him who is true. And we are in him who is true—even in his Son Jesus Christ. He is the true God and eternal life.

²¹Dear children, keep yourselves from idols.

5. With how much assurance can you say you "know that you have eternal life" (v. 13)?

6. What has the study of First John meant to you personally? What have you learned that has been of value to you?

7. On a scale of 1 (baby steps) to 10 (giant leaps), how has your relationship with God progressed over the last three months?

CARING TIME
(Answer all the questions that follow, then close in prayer.)

1. What will you remember most about this group?

2. What has the group decided to do next? What is the next step for you personally?

3. How would you like the group to continue to pray for you?

Notes—1 John 5:13–21

Summary. John concludes his epistle with some final comments which relate to the needs of his congregation. Now that his argument against the secessionists is over, John's style changes. He begins to speak more like a pastor than a polemicist. He now speaks directly to the needs of the congregations in Ephesus. In particular, he is anxious that they be encouraged. His encouragement comes in the form of a series of assurances. He begins by assuring them that they do have eternal life since they "believe in the name of the Son of God" (v. 13). He then assures them that God hears and answers prayer (vv. 14–17). Finally, writing in almost a poetic fashion, he assures them that they will be kept safe from a life of habitual sin (v. 18); that they are indeed children of God (v. 19); and that they do, indeed, know the truth (v. 20).

5:13–17 The previous passage ended with John pointing out that to possess the Son was to possess life and that those who do not possess the Son do not possess life (5:12). Just as he has done several times already in this letter when he has described both the positive and the negative side of an issue, he then hastens to reassure his readers that they are on the right side and so in no danger. In these verses he assures them that since they believe "in the name of the Son of God" they do, indeed, have eternal life.

> *Not only do Christians enjoy the assurance of eternal life, they have a second assurance: that God will answer their prayers.*

5:13 This verse parallels John 20:31 which is the concluding verse of the Gospel. (John 21 is an epilogue.) In his Gospel John writes: "But these are written that you may believe that Jesus is the Christ, the Son of God, and that by believing you may have life in his name." John wrote his Gospel in order to witness to Jesus and so inspire faith in those who did not yet know Christ. By believing in Jesus, they would discover "life." His purpose in the epistle is similar, except that now his words are directed to those who have, in fact, come to believe in Jesus.

His purpose is no longer to tell them how to find "life" but, instead, to assure them that they do have eternal life—no matter what the secessionists might say.

these things. John is referring back to the whole epistle and not just to the previous passage (5:1–12) as comparison with the parallel sentence in his Gospel shows. His words there, "But these [things] are written that you may believe ..." (John 20:31) are clearly a reference to all he has written in the Gospel just as here the phrase "these things" recalls all he has said in the epistle.

eternal life. The primary meaning of this phrase is not "that which lasts forever" (though this is implied). Rather, what is in view is the very life of God himself which is shared with Christians through Jesus Christ.

5:14–17 Not only do Christians enjoy the assurance of eternal life, they have a second assurance: that God will answer their prayers.

5:14 confidence. Originally this word meant "freedom of speech." It was used to describe the right of all those in a democracy to speak their mind. By this word John refers to the bold confidence Christians have—that they can approach God in prayer and freely speak their minds.

according to his will. In 3:22, John says that the condition for answered prayer is obedient behavior: we "receive from him [God] anything we ask, because we obey his commands and do what pleases him." Here John adds another condition: what we ask must be in accord with God's purposes (see also Matt. 26:39,42). "Prayer rightly considered is not a device for employing the resources of omnipotence to fulfill our own desires, but a means by which our desires may be redirected according to the mind of God, and made into channels for the forces of his will" (C.H. Dodd).

5:15 he hears us. By this phrase John means "he hears us favorably." To know that God hears is to know that "we have what we asked."

we have what we asked. "Our petitions are granted at once: the results of the granting are perceived in the future" (Plummer).

5:16 John now offers an illustration of how prayer operates. He is probably not using the term "brother" to refer to other Christians, but rather in the broader sense of "neighbors" or possibly even as "nominal church members." This is evident from how he writes about these people. He says that Christians ought to pray that God will give "life" to a "brother" whose sin "does not lead to death." This is not the prayer one prays for Christians who already have eternal life as John has just pointed out in verses 11–12. (This broader use of the word "brother" is also found in 3:16–17 as well as in Matt. 5:22–24 and 7:3–5.)

a sin that leads to death. Although John's readers probably understood what he was referring to, it is not at all clear to the modern reader just what this phrase means. A specific kind of sin is probably not in view here but rather a lifestyle of habitual, willing and persistent sinning. Perhaps what John has in mind are people like some of the Pharisees he and the other apostles encountered when they were with Jesus. These men saw Jesus' works and heard his words and yet still pronounced that he was empowered by Satan (Mark 3:22–30). To call good, evil, to understand light to be darkness, is evidence of a mindset that would never call upon God for forgiveness. And if one does not ask, forgiveness cannot be granted. And so one goes to death unrepentant and unforgiven.

I am not saying that he should pray about that. While John does not forbid prayer for those involved in a "sin that leads to death," he does not advise it since he doubts its value in such a case.

5:18 John concludes with a final list of assurances, written in almost poetic style. The first affirmation relates to Christian behavior: "It expresses the truth, not that he [the Christian] cannot ever slip into acts of sin, but rather that he does not persist in it habitually. ... The new birth results in new behavior. Sin and the child of God are incompatible. They may occasionally meet; they cannot live together in harmony" (Stott).

> The reason that Christians do not abide in sin is that they are kept safe by the power of Jesus Christ who has already destroyed the works of Satan.

the one who was born of God. By this phrase John refers to Jesus Christ. In the past he has referred to Christians in a similar way (2:29; 3:9; 4:7; 5:1,4). In other words, almost identical phrases are used to describe both the Christian and the Christ.

keeps him safe. The reason that Christians do not abide in sin is that they are kept safe by the power of Jesus Christ who has already destroyed the works of Satan (3:8). (See John 10:28; 17:12,15; 1 Peter 1:5 and Jude 24.)

5:19 The second affirmation which John makes is that they are, indeed, "children of God." They are part of the family of God and in relationship with the other children of God. This assertion comes in the form of a categorical statement: either a person is "of God" or a person is of "the world" and, as John has already shown, the world is under the control of Satan. John offers no third category. He assures those who are "born of God" (v. 18) that they are "children of God."

5:20 The third affirmation is that they really do know what is true (over against the secessionists who are promoting a new truth). John asserts this fact in several ways. First, the source of their insight is "the Son of God" who "has given us understanding." The purpose of this understanding is so that they can know "him who is true." Second, it is not just that in knowing Christ they accept his teachings to be true. It is deeper than that. They are "in him who is true." Truth is not something external. They are "in" the truth and the truth is "in them." Furthermore, to be in the Son is to be in the "true God" and share his very life.

has come and has given us understanding. By this phrase John highlights the two-fold work of Christ. He came—and thus provided salvation. But he also brought new understanding into the nature of God. Both redemption and revelation are central to the ministry of Jesus.

understanding. This is the power or ability to know what is actually so. Specifically, Jesus gave

Christians the power to perceive the true God as over against false idols (see v. 21).

5:21 *keep yourself.* This is not the same Greek word that is translated "keep" in verse 18. This word means "guard yourself." So what John is saying is that while Christ keeps the Christian safe (v. 18), so too, simultaneously, the Christian must work at staying away from Satan.

idols. Whether John has specific idols in mind is not clear. He may mean: "Do not abandon the real for the illusory" (Blaiklock). His imperative may refer either to the false images of the heretical teachers which created a form of idolatry or it may refer to the pagan idols that filled the city of Ephesus. Ephesus was the site of the great temple of Diana which was one of the wonders of the ancient world. It was also the site of immoral rites and the haunt of criminals (because they could not be arrested while in the temple). Its influence permeated the city.

Acknowledgments

In preparing notes such as these, there is a strong dependence upon the tools of New Testament research (e.g. the Arndt and Gingrich Greek-English Lexicon; Bible Dictionaries; New Testament Introductions; etc.). In addition, use has been made of various commentaries. While it is not possible as one would desire, given the scope and aim of this book, to acknowledge in detail the input of each author, the source of direct quotes and special insights is given. The three key commentaries that were used are: Raymond E. Brown, *The Epistles of John* (The Anchor Bible), Garden City, NY: Doubleday and Company, Inc., 1982; I. Howard Marshall, *The Epistles of John* (The New International Commentary on the New Testament), Grand Rapids: Wm. B. Eerdmans Publishing Co., 1978; and John R. W. Stott, *The Epistles of John* (Tyndale New Testament Commentaries), London: The Tyndale Press, 1964.

In addition, reference was made to William Barclay, *The Letters of John and Jude* (The Daily Study Bible), Edinburgh: The Saint Andrew Press, 1958; F. F. Bruce, *The Epistle of John*, Grand Rapids: Wm. B. Eerdmans Publishing Co., 1970; C. H. Dodd, *The Johannine Epistles* (MNTC), London: Hodder and Stoughton, 1946; Hass, deJonge, Swellongrebel, *A Translator's Handbook on the Letters of John*, London: United Bible Societies, 1972; J. L. Houlden, *A Commentary on the Johannine Epistles* (Harper's New Testament Commentaries), New York: Harper & Row, 1973; Marilyn Kunz and Catherine Schell, *1 John and James* (Neighborhood Bible Studies), Wheaton: Tyndale House Publishers, 1965; and Rodney A. Whitacre, *Johannine Polemic: The Role of Tradition and Theology* (SBL Dissertation Series 67), Chico, CA: Scholars Press, 1982.

Caring Time Notes